Remember This?

People, Things and Events
FROM **1948** TO THE **PRESENT DAY**

UK EDITION

With thanks for additional research by Dale Barham, Nicola Gardiner and Janice Morton.

Baby names: Office of National Statistics.

Cover images: Mary Evans – Illustrated London News Ltd, Francis Frith, Keystone Pictures USA/zumapress.com, aviation-images.com. Library of Congress – Balthazar Korab Collection LC-DIG-krb-00467. Cover icons from rawpixel/Freepik.

Cover Design: Fanni Williams / thehappycolourstudio.com

The Milestone Memories series including this *Remember This?* title is produced by Milestones Memories Press, a division of Say So Media Ltd.

First edition: October 2021
Updated: December 2022

We've tried our best to check our facts, but mistakes can still slip through. Spotted one? We'd love to know about it: info@saysomedia.net

Rewind, Replay, Remember

What can you remember before you turned six? If you're like most of us, not much: the comforting smell of a blanket or the rough texture of a sweater, perhaps. A mental snapshot of a parent arriving home late at night. A tingle of delight or the shadow of sorrow.

But as we grow out of childhood, our autobiographical and episodic memories – they're the ones hitched to significant events such as birthdays or leaving school – are created and filed more effectively, enabling us to piece them together at a later date. And the more we revisit those memories, the less likely we are to lose the key that unlocks them.

These fragments are assembled into a more-or-less coherent account of our lives – the one we tell ourselves, our friends, our relatives. And while this one-of-a-kind biopic loses a little definition over the years, some episodes remain in glorious technicolour – although it's often the most embarrassing incidents!

But this is one movie that's never quite complete. Have you ever had a memory spring back unbidden, triggered by something seemingly unrelated? This book is an attempt to discover those forgotten scenes using the events, sounds, and faces linked to the milestones in your life.

It's time to blow off the cobwebs and see how much you can remember!

It Happened in 1948

The biggest event in the year is one that didn't make the front pages: you were born! Here are some of the national stories that people were talking about.

+ London hosts first Summer Olympics since the war (right)
+ First post-war motor show held at London's Earls Court
+ Caribbean workers arrive in UK aboard Empire Windrush
+ Polo, 'the mint with the hole', goes on sale
+ Solihull-built off-roader the Land Rover unveiled
+ Electricity supply industry nationalised
+ Philosopher Bertrand Russell delivers first Reith Lecture
+ National Health Service established
+ BBC topical discussion show Any Questions? first broadcast
+ 12-year-old jockey Lester Piggott rides first winner
+ Co-op opens UK's first self-service supermarket in east London
+ Listed buildings act introduced to save architectural heritage
+ Bread rationing ends
+ Poor Law scrapped, ending the harsh workhouse system
+ British Railways formed to run nation's rail system
+ Heir to the throne Princes Charles born at Buckingham Palace
+ Laurence Olivier's Hamlet wins UK's first best picture Oscar
+ Poet TS Eliot awarded Nobel literature prize
+ Iron Age treasure hoard found at Snettisham, Norfolk
+ First Stoke Mandeville Games, Paralympics predecessor, held

Born this year:
& Singer Lulu born Marie McDonald McLaughlin Lawrie in Glasgow
& Irish republican politician Gerry Adams born in Belfast
& Led Zeppelin singer Robert Plant born in West Bromwich

Built as the Empire Stadium for the 1923 FA Cup Final, Wembley Stadium also hosted the 1948 Olympics – the first games held since 1936 and known as the 'Austerity Games'. Athletes were under rations like the rest of the population: they received the enhanced allowance given to miners and dockers. Around 85,000 packed Wembley for the opening ceremony; the running track was laid with cinders from Leicester's domestic hearths, chosen because of the quality of the coal burned there. Around 800 tons were transported by lorry to London.

On the Bookshelf When You Were Small

The books of our childhood linger long in the memory. These are the children's classics, all published in your first ten years. Do you remember the stories? What about the covers?

1949	The Secret Seven by Enid Blyton
1949	Amazon Adventure by Willard Price
1949	No Boats on Bannermere by Geoffrey Trease
1950	**Lion, Witch and Wardrobe by CS Lewis** Ten years in the writing, Lewis destroyed the first version of the book because his friends disliked it.
1950	First Book Ever by Richard Scarry
1950	**If I Ran the Zoo by Dr Seuss** Without this book, we would have no nerds: the word was coined by Seuss.
1952	Prince Caspian by CS Lewis
1952	**Charlotte's Web by EB White** Charlotte's full name is given as Charlotte A. Cavatica. This is derived from Araneus cavaticus, commonly known as the barn spider.
1952	The Borrowers by Mary Norton
1953	The Silver Chair by CS Lewis
1953	Down with Skool! by Geoffrey Willans
1954	The Eagle of the Ninth by Rosemary Sutcliff
1954	Horton Hears a Who! by Dr Seuss
1956	Kenny's Window by Maurice Sendak
1956	**Hundred and One Dalmatians by Dodie Smith** Dodie Smith wrote the book after one of her friends commented that her dalmatians would make a lovely coat. She had nine – including a Pongo.
1956	The Silver Sword by Ian Serraillier
1956	Little Old Mrs Pepperpot by Alf Prøysen
1957	Moominland Midwinter by Tove Jansson
1957	The Cat in the Hat by Dr Seuss
1958	Five Get into a Fix by Enid Blyton
1958	A Bear Called Paddington by Michael Bond

Around the World in Your Birth Year

Here are the events from abroad that were big enough to make news at home in the year you were born. And you won't remember any of them!

- ✦ South Africa names racial segregation policies Apartheid
- ✦ US launches V-2 rocket into space with monkey astronaut aboard
- ✦ US sexologist Alfred Kinsey publishes first human sexuality study
- ✦ American Broadcasting Corporation goes on air for first time
- ✦ Soviet forces leave North Korea
- ✦ Hindu extremist assassinates Mahatma Gandhi in New Delhi
- ✦ Ashgabat earthquake in Turkmenistan kills 110,000
- ✦ Hells Angels Motorcycle Club founded in Fontana, California
- ✦ British colonies Ceylon and Burma gain independence
- ✦ Swiss engineer George de Mestral invents Velcro
- ✦ Communists seize power in Czechoslovakia
- ✦ Columbia Records releases world's first long-playing record
- ✦ Republic of Korea formally established in southern Korea
- ✦ World Health Organisation set up to coordinate UN health affairs
- ✦ US agrees Marshall Plan to provide $17 billion in European aid
- ✦ Organisation for European Economic Co-operation formed
- ✦ Soviets blockade West Berlin; US and UK fly in food and fuel
- ✦ Costa Rica is first country to abolish its army
- ✦ United Nations adopts Universal Declaration of Human Rights
- ✦ State of Israel created – 200,000 European war refugees admitted

Born this year:
- US shock-rocker Alice Cooper born Vincent Damon Furnier in Detroit
- Fleetwood Mac singer Stevie Nicks born in Phoenix, Arizona
- Gallic actor Gérard Depardieu born in Châteauroux, France
- Singer Jimmy Cliff born James Chambers in Somerton, Jamaica

Boys' Names When You Were Born

Stuck for a name in the early 20th century? The answer was simple: use your own. Will nobody think of the genealogists? Here are the most popular names in England and Wales in 1948.

John

David

Michael

In America, it's said that 'everyone has an uncle Mike', such is the enduring appeal of Michael as a baby name in the 20th century. But third position in the forties is as good as it got here in the UK.

Peter

Robert

Anthony

Brian

Alan

William

James

Richard

Kenneth

Roger

Keith

Colin

Christopher

Raymond

Rising and falling stars:

Flash in the pan in this Top 100 was Melvyn at 78 (never seen again). Barrie, Reginald, Ernest and Edwin were also heading for the exit, while newcomers included Kevin, Nigel and Terry.

A note about other parts of the UK:

Baby name data isn't available until 1974 for Scotland and the turn of the century for Northern Ireland. How different are they? In the mid-seventies around a third of Scotland's Top 100 boys' names weren't in the English and Welsh equivalent – but the highest ranked of these was Gordon at number 30. By 2019, Scotland-only names ranked 4th (Harris), 7th (Lewis), 18th (Brodie), 22nd (Finlay) and more.

Girls' Names When You Were Born

Some parents pick names that are already popular. Others try to pick something more unusual – only to find out a few years later that thousands had the same idea.

Margaret
Patricia
Christine
Margaret, Christine and Patricia were all at peak popularity but nothing lasts forever: Margaret vanished first, then Patricia, and finally Christine in the mid-eighties.

Mary
Jean
Ann
Susan
Janet
Maureen
Barbara
Valerie
Carol
Sandra
Pauline
Elizabeth
Joan
Pamela
Jennifer
Kathleen
Anne
Sheila
Brenda
Gillian
Linda
Jacqueline

Rising and falling stars:
Blink and you miss it: Glenys and Vivienne were one-hit wonders. But Susan, Carol, Sandra, Linda and Diane would prove they had staying power. Goodbye Beryl, Norma, Cynthia, Mavis and Vera.

Things People Did When You Were Growing Up...

...that hardly anyone does now. Some of these we remember fondly; others are best left in the past!

- Use a mangle
- Do your National Service (it ended in 1960)
- **Use an outside toilet**
  Slum clearances and grants saw the end of most outside toilets, although in 2010 around 40,000 properties still had one.

- Take the trolley bus to school
- Fetch coal from the cellar
- Wear a hat to work
- **Use a coal tar vaporizer**
  A coal tar inhaler or vaporizer – probably made by Wright's, with the matching liquid – seemed like a good idea for treating whooping cough. It wasn't. A 1930s example held by the National Trust has a simple caption: 'This is poisonous.'

- Travel without a seatbelt
- **Rent a TV**
  When tellies cost a fortune (and frequently broke), renting a TV made sense. Where to go? Radio Rentals, who promised, 'You'll be glued to our sets, not stuck with them!'

- **Wear a housecoat**
  Who can think of a housecoat and curlers without remembering Coronation Street's Hilda Ogden?

- Scrub your doorstep
- Creosote the fence (banned for DIY in 2003)
- **Smoke a pipe**
  Stephen Fry was the last Pipe Smoker of the Year, in 2003.
- **Spank (or be spanked)**
  Corporal punishment ended in most schools in 1986. It is illegal in Scottish and Welsh homes, but not in England or N. Ireland.

- Pay the Pools collector
- Build a soapcart
- **Write a letter**
  Royal Mail still handles 10 billion letters each year but very few are handwritten. More than a fifth of UK children have never received a letter.

Old-fashioned Games

In a pre-digital age, boardgames ruled. Many of these predate you buy decades, centuries or more but still played; others gather dust in attics and charity shops.

1928	Escalado
1934	Sorry!
1935	**Monopoly** The origins of this stalwart lie with The Landlord's Game, an education tool patented in 1904 by Elizabeth Magie. (The anti-monopoly version – Prosperity – didn't catch on.) It was the first game to feature a never-ending path rather than a fixed start and finish.
1938	Buccaneer
1938	Scrabble
1935	Whot!
1947	Subbuteo
1949	**Cluedo** Cluedo, or Clue as it is known in the USA, introduced us to a host of shady country house characters and a selection of murder weapons. For years those included a piece of genuine lead pipe – thankfully replaced on health grounds.
1925	Dover Patrol
1851	**Happy Families** The original and much-copied Happy Families card game was launched for the Great Exhibition in 1851. For 20th Century children, Happy Families also means the million-selling book series by Allan Ahlberg, based loosely on the card game, which in turn inspired a BBC series.
1889	**Tiddlywinks** Trademarked as Tiddledy-Winks by Joseph Fincher, this much-maligned game has nevertheless found fans at elite universities, spawned countless spin-offs and rule variations (known in Tiddlywink parlance as 'perversions').
896	Ludo
892	Chinese Chequers
938	Totopoly
ancient gypt	Mancala

Things People Do Now...

...that were virtually unknown when you were young.
How many of these habits are part of your routine or even
second nature these days? Do you remember the first time?

+ Shop on Sunday (made possible in England and Wales in 1994)
+ Microwave a curry
+ **Leave a voicemail**
  At least you'll never have to change the cassette again!
+ **Watch last night's TV**
  Nowadays, you don't have to remember to set the VCR (and get a
  small child to help you do it). BBC iPlayer was the UK's first
  on-demand, streaming service, launched in 2007.

+ Strim grass
+ Change a fitted sheet
+ Recharge your toothbrush
+ Order a takeaway meal... to be delivered
+ Delete a photo
+ **Fit a disposable nappy**
  The first disposable 'napkins' went on sale in 1949 as two-part
  Paddis, invented by Valerie Hunter Gordon.

+ Eat an avocado
+ Use Google
+ Take a shower
+ **Make a video call (right)**
+ Buy a cheap flight
+ **Floss your teeth**
  Not a flosser? Take heart from a 2016 US research review:
  evidence for its benefit is very weak, and official advice to floss
  was dropped. Poking around with those pesky interdental
  brushes is how you should be spending your time (and money).

+ Pressure wash your patio
+ **Stick a self-adhesive stamp**
  You can probably still remember the taste of stamp glue, even
  though the sticky versions were introduced in 1993.

+ Answer an email (or send it to spam)
+ **Use a duvet**
  Sir Terence Conran is credited with finally persuading Brits to
  ditch the blankets when he introduced duvets in his Habitat
  stores in the sixties.

Zoom, Skype, FaceTime and more: if you weren't making face-to-face calls before the lockdowns of 2020, that's probably when you made your first. But it has taken 50 years to catch on and for technology to catch up: shown above is AT&T's PicturePhone, demonstrated in 1964 at New York's World's Fair. (The cost didn't help: renting a pair of devices for three minutes cost the equivalent of £100.)

Popular Food in the 1950s

Few would wish the return of fifties food, even the dishes introduced after rationing finally ended in 1954. Tinned food, stacked high. For flavour, take your pick: ketchup, brown sauce, or salad cream. Keep your olive oil in the bathroom cabinet. But a few favourites live on: who can resist a coronation chicken sandwich?

Milkshakes
Thick, creamy and an ideal hiding place for a lethal dose of poison. That's what the CIA thought when they plotted to slip a pill into Castro's beloved chocolate milkshake. Fortunately for the Cuban leader, the pill stuck to the freezer door.

Chop Suey

Real cream cakes

Bananas
In the 1950s, Gros Michel bananas – the dominant banana sold – were wiped out by the Panama disease, nearly destroying the banana industry.

Peaches

Frosties
Introduced in 1954 as Sugar Frosted Flakes, this new cereal was an instant hit – as was Tony the Tiger.

Frozen chicken

Tinned pineapple
Think pineapple, think Hawaii. Pineapples are still cultivated there, although the state's last cannery closed in 2006.

Spam fritters
Dubbed the 'Miracle Meat' when it was introduced in the late thirties, Spam is no longer made in the UK but it's still popular. Worldwide, around 7 billion cans have been sold; 44,000 cans are still produced every hour.

Baked Alaska

Devilled eggs

Coronation chicken

Hamburgers
In the US during WWII, hamburgers were briefly rebranded 'liberty steaks' in a renewed bout of food-as-propaganda. In World War I, sauerkraut was 'liberty cabbage' while French fries became 'freedom fries' during the Iraq war.

Pre-war Chocolate

Many of the chocolate bars we enjoy today were dreamed up long before WWII – though recipes, sizes and names have mostly been given a tweak or two over the decades to keep them as our newsagent favourites.

1800s	**Fry's Chocolate Cream** The first chocolate bars to be mass-produced.
1905	Cadbury Dairy Milk
1908	Bourneville
1914	Fry's Turkish Delight
1920	Flake
1926	Cadbury's Fruit & Nut
1927	**Jaffa Cake** Her Majesty's Customs and Excise tried to argue that a Jaffa Cake is a biscuit and subject to VAT. McVitie's won the day, in part because Jaffa cakes go hard when stale, unlike biscuits which go soft.
1929	Crunchie
1932	**Mars Bar** Want to buy a Mars bar in the US? Ask for a Milky Way.
1932	Penguin
1935	Aero
1935	**Milky Way** The Milky Way is not named after our galaxy, but instead after a type of malted milk, or milkshake as it's now known.
1936	Milky Bar
1937	**Kit Kat** Before Joseph Rowntree trademarked the term 'Kit Kat' in 1911 and the snack's eventual launch in the thirties, the name was most commonly associated with a mutton pie made by pastry chef Christopher Catt. He served it in his London Kit-Cat Club during the late 17th Century.
1937	Rolo
1939	**Marathon** In 1990, Marathon became Snickers: the US name since its 1930 launch (named after Frank Mars's horse). In the seventies, Mars sold a chocolate bar in the US called the Marathon – and it's still on sale here as the Curly Wurly.

Cars of the 1950s

Do you remember your first road trip? Bare legs welded to the hot plastic seats, buffeted by gusts of warm air through the open windows and not a seatbelt to be seen. There's a fair chance you'll have been cooped up in one of these fifties favourites.

Austin Westminster

Ford Prefect
In The Hitchhiker's Guide to the Galaxy, an arriving alien picks the name Ford Prefect thinking it would be inconspicuous.

Vauxhall Velox

Sunbeam Talbot

Rover 60

Ford Anglia
Features on the cover of Harry Potter and the Chamber of Secrets.

Ford Consul

Hillman Minx

Morris Minor
Originally named Mosquito, the name was changed at the last minute as it was feared that the name would deter conservative buyers. It went on to become the first million-selling British car.

MG Magnette

Morris Oxford

Singer Gazelle

Standard Vanguard
Named after a Navy battleship to appeal to ex-servicemen.

Austin Cambridge

Wolseley / Riley One Point Five
The Riley One Point Five and the Wolseley shared features including the engine, suspension and dimensions. The Riley was originally intended as a replacement for the Morris Minor.

Ford Popular

Land Rover
The first Land Rover was inspired by World War II jeeps, with the steering wheel in the middle. A Land Rover with tank tracks for agricultural work and a monster truck version followed.

Austin A30
Dubbed the steel teddy bear due to its rounded, cute appearance.

1958 brought a rather less welcome motoring innovation: the parking meter. The first meters installed in Mayfair, London (sixpence for an hour, a shilling for two), triggered the predictable result from day one: parked cars crammed onto neighbouring streets without restrictions, below.

The Biggest Hits When You Were 10

Whistled by your father, hummed by your sister or overheard on the radio, these are the hit records as you reached double digits.

Great Balls of Fire ♪ Jerry Lee Lewis
Jerry Lee Lewis infamously had to abandon a UK tour after word got out that he was married to his 13-year-old cousin, Myra Gale Brown.

Jailhouse Rock ♪ Elvis Presley
Among the most memorable covers of this Elvis classic is the one by Dan Aykroyd and John Belushi for the finale of the hit John Landis movie, The Blues Brothers.

The Story of My Life ♪ Michael Holliday
Magic Moments ♪ Perry Como
Whole Lotta Woman ♪ Marvin Rainwater
Who's Sorry Now ♪ Connie Francis

All I Have to Do Is Dream ♪ The Everly Brothers
All I Have to Do is Dream was written by the husband-and-wife songwriting partnership of Felice and Boudleaux Bryant, who wrote nearly 6,000 songs in their career.

When ♪ The Kalin Twins
Carolina Moon ♪ Connie Francis
It's All in the Game ♪ Tommy Edwards
Hoots Mon ♪ Lord Rockinghams XI

It's Only Make Believe ♪ Conway Twitty
Conway Twitty has been introduced to a whole new generation thanks to a running gag on Seth Macfarlane's adult cartoon show, Family Guy.

Tech Breakthroughs Before You Turned 21

Much of the technology we use today stands on the shoulders of the inventions made while you were small. Here are some of the most notable advances.

1948	Computer program
1950	Teleprompter
1951	Wetsuit
1953	Heart-lung machine
1955	Pocket transistor radio
1956	Hard Disk Drive
1956	Operating system (OS)
1957	**Laser** The strength of the first laser was measured in 'Gillettes', as scientists tested the laser by assessing how many Gillette razor blades it could slice.
1958	Microchip
1959	Xerox copier
1959	**Three-point seatbelt** The patented three-point safety belt was first installed by Volvo in 1959. Volvo waived the patent rights so other manufacturers could use the design for free.
1959	Weather satellite
1962	Red LEDs
1964	Plasma display
1965	Hypertext (http)
1966	Computer RAM
1967	Hand-held calculator
1967	**Computer mouse** Doug Engelbart patented an early version of his 'X-Y indicator' in 1967. By the time a (very large) mouse became available with a Xerox computer in 1981, the patent had expired.

On the Silver Screen When You Were 11

From family favourites to the films you weren't allowed to watch, these are the movies that drew the praise and crowds when you turned 11.

Jack the Ripper ✎ Lee Patterson, Eddie Byrne
I'm All Right Jack ✎ Ian Carmichael, Terry-Thomas
Look Back in Anger ✎ Richard Burton, Claire Bloom
The 39 Steps ✎ Robert Donat, Madeleine Carrol
North by Northwest ✎ Cary Grant, Eva Marie Saint
James Stewart thought he would be cast as Roger Thornhill. To avoid hurting his feelings, Hitchcock waited until he was committed to Anatomy of a Murder before casting Cary Grant.

Our Man in Havana ✎ Alec Guinness, Burl Ives
The Diary of Anne Frank ✎ Millie Perkins, Richard Beymer
Upstairs and Downstairs ✎ Michael Craig, Anne Heywood
Upstairs and Downstairs features the first English-language performance by Hollywood legend, Claudia Cardinale.

The Navy Lark ✎ Cecil Parker, Ronald Shiner
Suddenly, Last Summer ✎ Elizabeth Taylor, Montgomery Clift
Anatomy of a Murder ✎ James Stewart, Lee Remick
Expresso Bongo ✎ Laurence Harvey, Sylvia Syms
Some Like It Hot ✎ Marilyn Monroe, Tony Curtis
Curtis wasn't sure why Wilder wanted him. Wilder's response? 'You're the handsomest kid in town. Who else am I going to use?'

Ben-Hur ✎ Charlton Heston, Stephen Boyd
Ben-Hur caused a stir among animal rights activists. As many as 100 horses died during this epic film's production.

Operation Petticoat ✎ Cary Grant, Tony Curtis
Pillow Talk ✎ Rock Hudson, Doris Day
The Mouse That Roared ✎ Peter Sellers, Jean Seberg
The Devil's Disciple ✎ Burt Lancaster, Kirk Douglas
Room at the Top ✎ Laurence Harvey, Simone Signoret
Porgy and Bess ✎ Dorothy Dandridge, Sidney Poitier
Imitation of Life ✎ Lana Turner, John Gavin
Libel ✎ Olivia de Havilland, Dirk Bogarde
The Mummy ✎ Christopher Lee, Peter Cushing

Comics When You Were Small

Did you spend your childhood hopping from one foot to the other, longing for the next edition of your favourite comic to appear on the shelves? If so, these may be the titles you were waiting for.

The Hotspur ✲ (1933-1959)
The first-ever issues of the Hotspur were sold with a free black mask. The same mask was rebranded as the Whoopee Mask when it was given away with the Beano debut five years later.

Knockout ✲ (1939-1963)
Knockout Comics (or Knock-Out as they were originally known) ran for 24 years before merging into Valiant. However, the title was revived in 1971 (and the hyphen removed). Unlike most comics of the early 70s, every page was in colour.

Girl ✲ (1951-1964)
Boys Own ✲ (1879-1967)
The Eagle ✲ (1950-1969)
Robin ✲ (1953-1969)
Some of the most popular Robin comic strips included BBC children's characters Andy Pandy and the Flower Pot Men.

TV Comic ✲ (1951-1984)
Jack and Jill ✲ (1954-1985)
Tiger ✲ (1954-1985)
The Tiger comic strip character Roy Race was so popular, he eventually became the star of his own comic – Roy of the Rovers.

The Topper ✲ (1953-1990)
The Beezer ✲ (1956-1993)
For the first 25 years of its run, Beezer – companion to Topper – was printed in large-format A3.

Buster ✲ (1960-2000)
Bunty ✲ (1958-2001)
The Dandy ✲ (1937-2012)
Beano ✲ (1938-present)
The most valuable copies of the first issue of Beano fetch over £17,000 at auction. There are only 20 left in the world today.

Around the UK

Double digits at last: you're old enough to eavesdrop on adults and scan the headlines. These may be some of the earliest national news stories you remember.

+ Work on UK's first full-length motorway, the M1, begins
+ London Planetarium, Britain's first, opened by Prince Philip
+ Race riots rage in London's Notting Hill
+ Vivian Fuchs and team make first overland crossing of Antarctica
+ Donald Campbell sets world water-speed record at 248 mph
+ First vertical take-off and landing aircraft tested in Belfast
+ New Gatwick Airport opens after £7.8m renovation
+ Britain hands over control of Christmas Island to Australia
+ Direct dialling introduced for UK phones
+ UK-Iceland clash over fishing rights kicks off first Cod War
+ Eight Manchester United players killed in Munich air crash
+ First of Carry On comedies, Carry On Sergeant, screened
+ Life Peerage Act enables commoners and women to sit in the Lords
+ Britain's first parking meters installed in London's Mayfair
+ State Opening of Parliament televised for the first time
+ Campaign for Nuclear Disarmament launched in London
+ First Paddington bear book published
+ Giant panda Chi-Chi arrives at London Zoo
+ Mike Hawthorn becomes UK's first Formula 1 world champion
+ BBC debuts long-running shows Grandstand and Blue Peter
+ Presentation of debutantes at court ends

Born this year:
- Comedian and actor Lenny (Lenworth) Henry born in Dudley
- Wallace and Gromit animator Nick Park born in Preston
- Wuthering Heights singer Kate Bush born in Bexleyheath, Kent

UK Buildings

Some were loathed then, loved now; others, the reverse. Some broke new architectural ground, others helped to power a nation or entertain. All of them were built before you were 40.

1951	**Royal Festival Hall** Following the bombing of the Queen's Hall during the Blitz, London was left without a major concert hall. The foundation stone was laid by PM Clement Attlee in 1949.
1961	**Dungeness Lighthouse** When you build a nuclear power station that blocks out the view of a lighthouse, what do you do? Build another one.
1961	**Guildford Cathedral** Scenes from 1976 film The Omen were shot here; cathedral staff had to encourage the locals to attend after filming.
1961	Park Hill, Sheffield
1962	Coventry Cathedral
1964	**Post Office Tower** The tower was previously a designated secret under the Official Secrets Act and didn't appear on any OS maps. It was a pretty prominent secret, though, and was used as a filming location for TV and film during this time.
1966	Birmingham GPO Tower
1966	Centre Point
1966	**Severn Bridge** Grade I listed, and since 2018, free to cross (both ways!).
1967	Queen Elizabeth Hall
1974	**Birmingham Library** Looked like 'a place where books are incinerated, not kept' said Prince Charles. It was demolished in 2013.
1976	National Exhibition Centre (NEC)
1976	**Brent Cross Centre** The UK's first American-style indoor shopping centre. The car park was used for the James Bond film Tomorrow Never Dies.
1980	NatWest Tower
1982	Barbican Centre
1986	Lloyd's Building

Early Radio 1 DJs

Do you remember the first time you heard 'the exciting new sound of Radio 1'? Replacing the BBC Light Programme in 1967, it soon won over the UK's youth to become the world's most popular station, and the DJs – all men until Annie Nightingale joined in 1970 – became household names.

Tony Blackburn
The man who started it all with those immortal words and span the first disc (Flowers in the Rain, by The Move). And don't forget his canine co-presenter, Arnold.

John Peel
Peel's life-long service to music is well known. But before this took off, his aspiration to be a journalist while selling insurance in Texas led him to bluff his way into the midnight news conference where Lee Harvey Oswald was paraded before the press.

Keith Skues

Ed Stewart
For children of the seventies, Ed Stewart means Crackerjack; but for those of us born earlier, it was Junior Choice on Saturday mornings where we'd get to know 'Stewpot'.

Mike Raven

Jimmy Young

Dave Cash

Kenny Everett
Everett was a Radio 1 DJ for less than three years before being sacked. He also appeared in 1980 on Just a Minute and was given the subject of marbles. Nicholas Parsons let him talk (while hesitating, repeating *and* deviating) for 90 seconds as a joke – assisted by the other panellists. He wasn't on the show again.

Terry Wogan

Duncan Johnson

Tommy Vance

Emperor Rosko
'Your groovy host from the West coast, here to clear up your skin and mess up your mind. It'll make you feel good all over!' – Rosko, aka Mike Pasternak, introducing his Midday Spin show.

Pete Murray

Bob Holness

Female Wimbledon Winners

Aged 15 in 1887, Lottie Dod was the youngest to win Wimbledon. Aged 37 in 1908, Charlotte Cooper Sterry was the oldest. These are the winners when you too were still in with a (slim) chance! Men, PTO!

1963	Margaret Smith
1964	**Maria Bueno** Bueno caused controversy by wearing a white dress with a pink underskirt, drawing grasps from the crowd.
1965	Margaret Smith
1966-68	**Billie Jean King** King lobbied for equal pay, won the Battle of the Sexes against Bobby Riggs and was the first woman to be chosen as Sports Illustrated's Sportsperson of the Year.
1969	Ann Jones
1970	Margaret Court
1971	Evonne Goolagong
1972-73	Billie Jean King
1974	Chris Evert
1975	Billie Jean King
1976	Chris Evert
1977	**Virginia Wade** Wade competed at Wimbledon 15 times before winning. It was to be Britain's last female grand slam victory until Emma Raducanu's epic US Open win in 2021.
1978-79	Martina Navratilova
1980	Evonne Goolagong Cawley
1981	**Chris Evert Lloyd** Nicknamed the Ice Maiden, Evert was the first tennis player to win 1,000 matches and the first female tennis player to reach $1million in career prize money.
982-87	Martina Navratilova

Wimbledon: The Men

In the men's tournament, Becker won at the tender age of 17. At the top end, Federer won in 2017 at the age of 35. But in 1909, in the amateur era, Arthur Gore was a nimble 41 years young – giving us our 'winning window' of 17 to 41.

1964-65	Roy Emerson
1966	Manuel Santana
1967	John Newcombe
1968-69	Rod Laver
1970-71	John Newcombe
1972	**Stan Smith** Outside tennis, Stan Smith is best known for his best-selling line of Adidas sports shoes.
1973	Jan Kodeš
1974	Jimmy Connors
1975	**Arthur Ashe** Ashe contracted HIV from a blood transfusion following a heart operation, and worked to raise the awareness of HIV and AIDS before his death at the age of 49. The Arthur Ashe Stadium in New York was named in his memory.
1976-80	Björn Borg
1981	John McEnroe
1982	Jimmy Connors
1983-84	John McEnroe
1985-86	**Boris Becker** As a child, Becker would sometimes practice with Steffi Graf. He dropped out of school to join the West German Tennis Federation.
1987	Pat Cash
1988	Stefan Edberg
1989	Boris Becker

Books of the Decade

Ten years that took you from kids' adventure books to dense works of profundity – or maybe just grown-up adventures! How many did you read when they were first published?

| 1958 | Things Fall Apart by Chinua Achebe |
| 1958 | **Breakfast at Tiffany's by Truman Capote** |

Holly Golightly was originally called Connie Gustafson. Capote hand-edited every instance, and also toned down the explicit conversations between Holly and Mag Wildwood.

1959	The Tin Drum by Günter Grass
1959	The Naked Lunch by William S Burroughs
1959	Cider with Rosie by Laurie Lee
1960	**To Kill a Mockingbird by Harper Lee**

The story was turned down by several publishers. Lee was so frustrated that she threw it out of her apartment window. She doubted that the book would have any success, but it continues to sell a million copies a year.

| 1961 | **Catch-22 by Joseph Heller** |

The book was originally titled Catch-18 but was changed due to its similarity to the title of the novel Mila 18, which had just been announced.

| 1961 | A House for Mr. Biswas by V S Naipaul |
| 1962 | **A Clockwork Orange by Anthony Burgess** |

Burgess was diagnosed with a brain tumour and wrote five novels in a year to provide his wife with income. It turned out to be a misdiagnosis; he lived for another 30 years.

1962	The Golden Notebook by Doris Lessing
1963	Cat's Cradle by Kurt Vonnegut
1963	V by Thomas Pynchon
1964	Herzog by Saul Bellow
1964	Last Exit to Brooklyn by Hubert Selby
1965	Dune by Frank Herbert
1966	Wide Sargasso Sea by Jean Rhys
1966	The Jewel In The Crown by Paul Scott
1967	One Hundred Years of Solitude by Gabriel Garcia Marquez
1967	The Outsiders by SE Hinton

Around the UK

Here's a round-up of the most newsworthy events from across the country in the year you turned (sweet) 16.

- ✦ Peter Allen and Gwynne Evans last men to be hanged in UK
- ✦ BBC2 begins broadcasting with episode of Play School
- ✦ ITV's motel soap opera Crossroads takes to the screens
- ✦ Pirate radio station Caroline begins broadcasting offshore
- ✦ First edition of The Sun rolls off the press
- ✦ Great Train robbers jailed for total of 307 years
- ✦ Roald Dahl's Charlie and the Chocolate Factory published
- ✦ Milton Keynes, Havant and Basingstoke 'new towns' proposed
- ✦ Mods and Rockers battle it out on Brighton beach
- ✦ TV chart show Top of The Pops first airs on BBC
- ✦ Innovative design firm Habitat opens its first store in London
- ✦ The Queen opens Forth Road bridge to traffic
- ✦ Malta gains its independence from Britain
- ✦ Labour's Harold Wilson becomes prime minister
- ✦ Elizabeth Taylor and Richard Burton wed in Montreal (right)
- ✦ Girls' teen magazine Jackie first published
- ✦ The Beatles first film A Hard Day's Night released
- ✦ Government votes to abolish death penalty for murder
- ✦ Construction of London's Post Office Tower completed
- ✦ UK and French governments agree to build Channel Tunnel
- ✦ British Northern Rhodesia becomes Republic of Zambia

Born this year:
- ⚭ Prince Edward, Earl of Essex, born in Buckingham Palace
- ⚭ Actress and comedian Kathy Burke born in Camden, London
- ⚭ UKIP leader and MEP Nigel Farage born in Farnborough, Kent

'Erotic vagrancy' was the charge from the Vatican when paparazzi photos of Elizabeth Taylor and Richard Taylor confirmed the rumours: she was dating a married man. He would soon be the fifth husband to the highest paid movie star in the world (and also the sixth, after their divorce and remarriage).

TV Newsreaders: The Early Days

Trusted, familiar, and mostly with received pronunciation: these are the faces that brought you and your family the news, and the dates they shuffled their papers.

Richard Baker 📺 (1954-82)
In 1954, Baker introduced the BBC's first TV news broadcast. Seventies children know his voice as the narrator of Mary, Mungo and Midge.

Robert Dougall 📺 (1955-73)
Kenneth Kendall 📺 (1955-69)
Angela Rippon 📺 (1975-2002)
The UK's first regular female newsreader and known nationwide for her 1976 Morecambe and Wise appearance.

Jill Dando 📺 (1988-99)
The shocking murder of Dando on her doorstep in 1999 remains unsolved.

Moira Stuart 📺 (1981-2007)
Peter Woods 📺 (1964-81)
Woods is the biological father of BBC journalist and presenter Justin Webb.

Nan Winton 📺 (1960-61)
Winton was the BBC's first on-screen female newsreader in a shortlived 1960 trial deemed unacceptable by viewers.

Reginald Bosanquet 📺 (1967-79)
Michael Aspel 📺 (1960-68)
Corbet Woodall 📺 (1963-67)
Anna Ford 📺 (1976-2006)
Jan Leeming 📺 (1980-87)
Lynette Lithgow 📺 (1988-96)
Selina Scott 📺 (1980-86)
Sue Lawley 📺 (1981-88)
Alongside her news duties, Lawley is best known for her 18-year stint presenting BBC Four's Desert Island Discs. She left the role in 2006.

Julia Somerville 📺 (1983-99)

Fifties TV Gameshows

Gameshows got off to a rocky start in the UK, but the advent of commercial TV in 1955 – and ad-funded prizes – boosted the format into primetime, where it has remained ever since. Many of these early shows have since been remade, but how many of the originals do you remember?

Tell the Truth

Twenty Questions
Host Gilbert Harding, dubbed by the BBC as Britain's 'best-loved and best-hated man', was particularly drunk during one recording. He insulted two of the panellists, caused chaos by failing to recognise an answer, and ended the show early. Read more about Harding on page 36.

What's My Line?
Arguably the nation's first TV gameshow, first on screens in 1951.

Round Britain Quiz

Top of the Form

Twenty-One

Beat the Clock

Concentration

Crackerjack

Do You Trust Your Wife?

Double Your Money
In 1959, Sir Bobby Charlton appeared as a contestant on the show and won the top prize of £1,000, answering questions on pop music. Dame Maggie Smith also appeared as a hostess for a short time before her acting career took off.

Name That Tune

Opportunity Knocks

Spot the Tune

Take Your Pick!
Take Your Pick! was the first gameshow to be broadcast on commercial TV, debuting on the newly launched ITV in 1955. The income generated by adverts made it the first UK gameshow to give away cash prizes.

Two for the Money

Keep it in the Family

Make Up Your Mind

Stamps When You Were Young

Stamp collecting was the first serious hobby for many 20th century children. Commemorative issues weren't issued until the twenties, but soon became highly collectible – and the perfect gift for uncles in need of inspiration. These stamps may well have started your collection.

1924-5	**British Empire Exhibition** Designed to showcase Britain's strengths in an era of declining global influence, the exhibition left a legacy: the Empire Stadium (later renamed Wembley Stadium). The stamps were the UK's first commemorative issue, sixty years after the USA did the same.
1929	**9th Universal Postal Union Congress, London** Arguably of little interest to few outside philatelic circles, this was the first of several self-referential issues over successive decades. See also the Inter-Parliamentary stamps first issued in 1957.
1935	George V Silver Jubilee
1937	George VI Coronation
1940	**Centenary of the first adhesive postage stamp** Everyone has heard of the first adhesive stamp, issued in 1840: the Penny Black. (Perforations didn't come along until the 1854 Penny Red.) The glue on commemorative stamps contained around 14 calories!
1946	Victory
1948	Royal Silver Wedding
1948	Olympic Games
1949	The 75th Anniversary of the Universal Postal Union
1951	Festival of Britain
1951	George VI (high value 'definitives')
1953	The coronation of Queen Elizabeth II
1955	Castles (high value 'definitives')
1957	**World Scout Jamboree** Held in Sutton Coldfield; 50,000 Scouts attended. After heavy rain, the US Air Force was called in to help.
1957	46th Inter-Parliamentary Union Conference
1958	6th British Empire and Commonwealth Games

The Biggest Hits When You Were 16

The songs that topped the charts when you turned 16 might not be in your top 10 these days, but you'll probably remember them!

Glad All Over ♪ The Dave Clark Five
Needles and Pins ♪ The Searchers
Anyone Who Had a Heart ♪ Cilla Black
Can't Buy Me Love ♪ The Beatles
It's Over ♪ Roy Orbison
House of the Rising Sun ♪ The Animals
A folk song, recorded by an electric rock band:
this was the song which convinced Bob Dylan to abandon
his roots and go electric.

It's All Over Now ♪ The Rolling Stones
A Hard Day's Night ♪ The Beatles
A Hard Day's Night was the feature song from The Beatles'
movie of the same name – their first motion picture.
It was a commercial success despite low expectations and a
correspondingly low budget.

Do Wah Diddy Diddy ♪ Manfred Mann
You Really Got Me ♪ The Kinks
I'm Into Something Good ♪ Herman's Hermits
Oh, Pretty Woman ♪ Roy Orbison
The track found a new lease of life when it was used as the
theme for Julia Robert's iconic movie, Pretty Woman nearly
30 years later.

Baby Love ♪ The Supremes
Little Red Rooster ♪ The Rolling Stones
Little Red Rooster was the first big hit for The Stones, but
was actually a cover of a song by one of their blues heroes,
Howlin' Wolf.

Household Goods in 1956

In 1947, the government calculated inflation for the first time using a basket of frequently purchased goods. This list has been reviewed ever since; the changes mirror our ever-changing tastes and habits. Here's what housewives were buying when you were small.

Youth club admission
Crispbread
Luncheon meat
Rice

NHS prescription
The controversial one shilling charge was introduced in 1952, prompting NHS founder Aneurin Bevan to resign. Prime Minister Harold Wilson abolished the prescription charge in 1965, before reintroducing it in 1968, with some exemptions.

Meat extracts
Plastic emulsion paint
TV tube replacement
Electric lamp
Cardigan
Tweed sports coat

Corset
Impractical corsets took a dive in popularity during the first half of the 20th century but experienced a resurgence during the 1950s when Christian Dior's 'new look' became fashionable.

Cat food
Smocked frock
Motor insurance

Driving test fee
In 1956, the driving test fee doubled to £1 before being suspended due to the Suez crisis. In 1957, three-year driving licences were introduced (and lasted until licenses were extended in 1976).

Dance hall admission
By 1953, dance halls were second in only to cinema. Around 70% of couples at the time are said to have met on the dance floor.

Camera film
Telegram

Blockbuster Movies When You Were 16

These are the movies that everyone was talking about. How many of them did you see (or have you seen since)?

A Fistful of Dollars 💷 Clint Eastwood, John Wells
The Train 💷 Burt Lancaster, Paul Scofield
Seven Days in May 💷 Burt Lancaster, Kirk Douglas
Nothing But the Best 💷 Alan Bates, Denholm Elliott
Dr Strangelove 💷 Peter Sellers, George C Scott
Night Must Fall 💷 Albert Finney, Mona Washbourne
Zulu 💷 Michael Caine, Stanley Baker
The Zulu extras had never seen a film before. The crew set up screenings to give an idea of what was required.

The Night of the Iguana 💷 Richard Burton, Ava Gardner
Mary Poppins 💷 Julie Andrews, Dick Van Dyke
Many of the nannies lining up for an interview in one of the earlier scenes were actually men in drag.

Becket 💷 Richard Burton, Peter O'Toole
The System 💷 Oliver Reed, Jane Merrow
The Pawnbroker 💷 Rod Steiger, Geraldine Fitzgerald
A Hard Day's Night 💷 John Lennon, Paul McCartney
The Killers 💷 Lee Marvin, Angie Dickinson
Carry On Cleo 💷 Sid James, Kenneth Williams
Goldfinger 💷 Sean Connery, Honor Blackman
Connery injured his back during the fight scene with Oddjob. He proceeded to use the injury to get a better deal on his next 007 feature.

The Leather Boys 💷 Rita Tushingham, Colin Campbell
Red Desert 💷 Monica Vitti, Richard Harris
The Masque of the Red Death 💷 Vincent Price, Jane Asher
The Pumpkin Eater 💷 Anne Bancroft, Peter Finch
Zorba the Greek 💷 Anthony Quinn, Irene Papas
The Third Secret 💷 Stephen Boyd, Pamela Franklin
King & Country 💷 Dirk Bogarde, Tom Courtenay
My Fair Lady 💷 Audrey Hepburn, Rex Harrison
Hepburn's singing voice caused so much concern the filmmakers dubbed 95% of her musical performances.

Gameshow Hosts of the Fifties and Sixties

Many of these men were semi-permanent fixtures, their voices and catchphrases almost as familiar as our family's. Some were full-time entertainers, born to the stage; others seemed rather less suited to the spotlight!

Ted Ray... ►◄ (Joker's Wild)
and his son, Robin Ray ►◄ (Face the Music)
Peter Wheeler ►◄ (Crossword on Two, Call My Bluff)
Robert Robinson ►◄ (Brain of Britain, Ask the Family)
McDonald Hobley ►◄ (Come Dancing, It's a Knockout)
David Jacobs ►◄ (Juke Box Jury)
Shaw Taylor ►◄ (Password, Pencil and Paper)
Eamonn Andrews ►◄ (Crackerjack!)
Roy Plomley ►◄ (Many a Slip)
Gilbert Harding ►◄ (Twenty Questions, What's My Line?)
Harding was a teacher and policeman before working in radio and television. Resentful of his fame, Harding was once left mortified on the London Underground when he was recognised by fellow passengers who failed to notice that TS Eliot was also in the same carriage.

Bamber Gascoigne ►◄ (University Challenge)
Tommy Trinder ►◄ (Sunday Night at the Palladium)
Bruce Forsyth ►◄ (Beat the Clock)
Bruce Forsyth first appeared on television in 1939. He had many talents including playing the ukulele and accordion, singing, dancing and acting. In his later years, Forsyth stated that he regretted presenting so many gameshows.

Leslie Crowther ►◄ (Billy Cotton Band Show, Crackerjack)
Bob Monkhouse ►◄ (The Golden Shot)
While serving in the RAF, Bob Monkhouse drafted a letter to the BBC from his group captain, stating that 18-year-old Monkhouse was a war hero and deserved an audition. His group captain signed the letter without reading it; Monkhouse got his audition.

Hughie Green ►◄ (Opportunity Knocks)
Derek Batey ►◄ (Mr and Mrs)
Wilfred Pickles ►◄ (radio show Have a Go)

Kitchen Inventions

The 20th-century kitchen was a playground for food scientists and engineers with new labour-saving devices and culinary shortcuts launched every year. Here are some your parents – and now you – wouldn't be without.

1929	**Dishwasher** The first hand-operated dishwasher was created in 1885 by inventor and socialite, Josephine Cochrane, who was tired of her servants chipping her fine china. In 1929, Miele brought out an electric, top-loading model. Front-loading and drying functions followed in 1940; automation in 1960.
1937	Blender
1939	Pressure cooker
1940	Chest freezer
1945	**Fridge** If you think today's American-style fridges are big, consider the Large Hadron Collider in Geneva. With a circumference of 17 miles and 9,300 magnets, it's chilled to -270C before use. That would definitely keep your milk cold.
1948	Kenwood mixer
1955	Automatic kettle
1956	**Non-stick pan** You can thank a French angler's wife for your non-stick pans: it was she who noticed her husband's habit of coating his gear in non-stick Teflon, and suggested he did the same to her pans. Scrambled egg fans owe her a life-long debt.
1960	**Tupperware** In 1960, Tupperware parties arrived in the UK. Earl Tupper's 1948 invention took off when a US single mother called Brownie Wise started home sales and the social selling concept proved equally successful here. This icon of female entrepreneurship was dismissed in 1958 for being too outspoken.
1974	Microwave
1974	Food processor
1976	**Deep fat fryer** The Egyptians, Romans and Greeks were all known to have been keen on deep frying their food – often items that look uncommonly like today's doughnuts (minus the jam).

Around the World When You Turned 18

These are the headlines from around the globe as you were catapulted into adulthood.

✦ Soviet spacecraft Venera 7 crashes on Venus
✦ US courts rule police must read rights before questioning
✦ India and Pakistan sign Tashkent peace accord
✦ First US Kwanzaa week honours African-American culture
✦ US bans possession, use and research on drug LSD
✦ Soviets successfully land unmanned spacecraft Luna 9 on Moon
✦ Boeing 707s crash into Mont Blanc and Mount Fuji, killing 15
✦ Musical The Sound of Music wins Best Picture Oscar
✦ Sci-fi series Star Trek boldly airs on US TV
✦ Barbados gains independence from Britain
✦ England beats West Germany to win World Cup for first time
✦ South African prime minister Verwoerd stabbed to death
✦ South American colony Guyana gains independence from UK
✦ US ups troops in Vietnam to 500,000 as war escalates
✦ UK's giant panda Chi Chi flies to USSR for mate-date
✦ Indira Gandhi elected as India's first female prime minister
✦ Military coups take place in Nigeria, Ghana and Upper Volta
✦ Mao Zedong launches Cultural Revolution to get rid of rivals

Born this year:
⚭ US supermodel Cindy Crawford born in DeKalb, Illinois
⚭ US boxing heavyweight champ Mike Tyson born in New York
⚭ Olympic runner Zola Budd born in Bloemfontein, South Africa

FA Cup Winners Since You Were Born

Many fans have waited decades to see their team lift the cup; many more are still waiting. Here are the teams that have hoisted the trophy in your lifetime (last win in brackets).

Blackpool ⚽ (1952-53)
Newcastle United ⚽ (1954-55)
Aston Villa ⚽ (1956-57)
After Aston Villa won the final in 1895, the FA Cup was stolen from a shop window display in Birmingham. The thief confessed 63 years later, stating he had melted the trophy down to make coins.

Bolton Wanderers ⚽ (1957-58)
Nottingham Forest ⚽ (1958-59)
Wolverhampton Wanderers ⚽ (1959-60)
West Bromwich Albion ⚽ (1967-68)
Leeds United ⚽ (1971-72)
Sunderland ⚽ (1972-73)
Southampton ⚽ (1975-76)
Ipswich Town ⚽ (1977-78)
West Ham United ⚽ (1979-80)
Coventry City ⚽ (1986-87)
Wimbledon ⚽ (1987-88)
Wimbledon shocked the country in 1988 when they beat First Division champions Liverpool in the FA Cup final, overcoming 17-1 odds.

Tottenham Hotspur ⚽ (1990-91)
Everton ⚽ (1994-95)
Portsmouth ⚽ (2007-08)
Wigan Athletic ⚽ (2012-13)
Manchester United ⚽ (2015-16)
Chelsea ⚽ (2017-18)
Former Chelsea and Ivory Coast striker Didier Drogba is the only player to score in four separate FA Cup Finals.

Manchester City ⚽ (2018-19)
Arsenal ⚽ (2019-20)
Leicester City ⚽ (2020-21)
Liverpool ⚽ (2021-22)

Around the UK

Voting. Placing a bet. Buying a legal drink. Turning 18 is serious stuff. Here's what everyone was reading about in the year you reached this milestone.

✦ Election triumph returns Labour prime minister Harold Wilson
✦ Satirical comedy show The Frost Report first show on BBC TV
✦ Kray Twins questioned over East End murder
✦ World Cup trophy stolen; later found by Pickles the dog
✦ Regular cross-Channel hovercraft service introduced
✦ Longleat estate opens UK's first drive-through safari park
✦ £1.5m of art stolen from London's Dulwich gallery
✦ Dounreay atomic power station opens in northern Scotland
✦ Moors Murderers Ian Brady and Myra Hindley jailed for life
✦ Soviet spy George Blake escapes from Wormwood Scrubs
✦ UK ceases all trade with Rhodesia
✦ Ken Loach's docudrama Cathy Come Home airs on BBC TV
✦ Bechuanaland (now Botswana) gains independence from UK
✦ Spoil tip avalanche kills 116 children in Aberfan, Wales (right)
✦ England beats Germany 4-2 to win World Cup at Wembley
✦ Action Man toy figure goes on sale
✦ John Lennon says Beatles 'are more popular than Jesus'
✦ Barclays Bank launches first British credit card
✦ South American colony Guyana gains independence from UK
✦ Pirate radio ship Caroline runs aground
✦ Severn Bridge opens connecting England and Wales

Born this year:
⚭ TV chef and restaurateur Gordon Ramsay born in Johnstone
⚭ Rugby player Martin Offiah born in Hackney, London
⚭ Actress Helena Bonham Carter born in Islington, London
⚭ Canadian actor Kiefer Sutherland born in London, UK

116 children, 28 adults: the almost unbearable toll of the Aberfan disaster.
At 0920 on Friday 21 October 1966, the fears of councillors, engineers and
more were realised: the tip that towered above Pantglas Junior School slipped.
The ensuing tragedy was beyond anyone's imagination as slurry travelling at 50
mph engulfed the children and teachers on their last morning before half term.
8 children were injured; only 10 were pulled alive from the hardening muck.
For survivors the psychological toll was to last a lifetime – compounded by the
National Coal Board's ineptitude, lack of accountability, late capitulation in the
inquiry and misuse of appeal funds. Many victims of Aberfan died; others lived.

Medical Advances Before You Were 21

A girl born in the UK in 1921 had a life expectancy of 59.6 years (boys: 55.6). By 2011 that was up to 82.8 (79 for boys), thanks to medical advances including many of these.

1949	Intraocular lens (myopia and cataracts)
1950	**Polio vaccine** In a TV interview, Jonas Salk was asked about taking a patent on the vaccine. He replied, 'Can you patent the sun?'
1951	Munchausen syndrome (described)
1952	**Artificial heart** The first artificial heart was built by General Motors. Before the operation, the patient saw two dogs with shaved chests running around, and discovered that they had been the final test subjects. The patient survived the procedure too.
1953	Ultrasound
1956	Paracetamol
1957	EEG topography (toposcope)
1958	Pacemaker
1959	Bone marrow transplant, in-vitro fertilisation
1960	Kidney transplant, CPR and coronary artery bypass surgery
1961	The pill
1962	Hip replacement, beta blockers
1963	**Valium** Valium was famously dubbed 'mother's little helper' by The Rolling Stones. Valium was hailed as a wonder drug as it worked was a far less risky alternative to barbiturates.
1963	Lung transplant, artificial heart
1964	Measles vaccine
1965	**Portable defibrillator** CPR on TV is successful one time in two, a 2009 study found: roughly the same as reality. However, the lack of follow-up or age-related differences on TV means people's expectation for a life-saving result is unrealistically high.
1966	Pancreas transplant
1967	Heart transplant

Popular Girls' Names

If you started a family at a young age, these are the names you're most likely to have chosen. And even if you didn't pick them, a lot of British parents did!

Susan
Julie
Karen
Jacqueline
Deborah
Tracey
Tracey, or Tracy? No matter, they're both in vogue (though not for long: they're gone by the eighties).

Jane
Helen
Diane
Sharon
Tracy
Angela
Sarah
Alison
Caroline
Amanda
Sandra
Linda
Catherine
Elizabeth
Carol
Joanne
Wendy
Janet
Dawn
Christine

Rising and falling stars:
Huge changes are afoot here, as for society at large:
a third of names make their last appearance including
Pamela, Carole, Pauline, Annette and Shirley. Shorter names
are in: Kim, Lisa, Sara and more.

Animals Extinct in Your Lifetime

Billions of passenger pigeons once flew the US skies.
By 1914, they had been trapped to extinction. Not every
species dies at our hands, but it's a sobering roll-call.
(Date is year last known alive or declared extinct).

1949	Sinú parakeet, Colombia
1951	Yemen gazelle
1952	**Deepwater cisco fish, USA** The deepwater cisco, once found in two Michigan lakes, was overfished and crowded out by invasive parasites and herring. Result? Extinction.
1952	San Benedicto rock wren, Mexico
1960	Candango mouse, Brasilia
1962	Red-bellied opossum, Argentina
1963	Kākāwahie honeycreeper, Hawaii
1964	South Island snipe, New Zealand
1966	Arabian ostrich
1967	Saint Helena earwig
1967	**Yellow blossom pearly mussel, USA** Habitat loss and pollution proved terminal for this resident of Tennessee.
1968	Mariana fruit bat (Guam)
1971	Lake Pedder earthworm, Tasmania
1972	Bushwren, New Zealand
1977	Siamese flat-barbelled catfish, Thailand
1979	Yunnan Lake newt, China
1981	Southern gastric-brooding frog, Australia
1986	Las Vegas dace
1989	Golden toad (see right)
2000	**Pyrenean ibex, Iberia** For a few minutes in 2003 this species was brought back to life through cloning, but sadly the newborn ibex died.
2001	Caspian tiger, Central Asia
2008	Saudi gazelle
2012	**Pinta giant tortoise** The rarest creature in the world for the latter half of his 100-year life, Lonesome George lived out his days in the Galapagos as the last remaining Pinta tortoise.

The observed history of the golden toad is brief and tragic. It wasn't discovered until 1964, abundant in a pristine area of Costa Rica. By 1989 it had gone, a victim of rising temperatures.

Popular Boys' Names

Here are the top boys' names for this year. In many instances it's merely a reshuffle of the popular names from the previous decade; but in the lower reaches, change is afoot…

David
Paul
Andrew
Mark
John
Michael
Stephen
Ian
Robert
Richard
Christopher
Peter
Simon
Anthony
Kevin
Gary

Steven
Steven stormed the Top 100 in the fifties and reached his peak here at 17. While all around him rose and fell, Steven stayed put for thirty long years.

Martin
James
Philip
Alan
Neil
Nigel
Timothy
Colin
Graham

Rising and falling stars:
Plenty of snappy new entrants here including Sean, Carl, Wayne and Dean. Multisyllabic Jeffrey (and Geoffrey), Vincent, Douglas and Francis enjoyed their last outing.

Popular Movies When You Were 21

The biggest stars in the biggest movies: these are the films the nation was enjoying as you entered adulthood.

Sweet Charity 🎬 Shirley MacLaine, John McMartin
Till Death Do Us Part 🎬 Warren Mitchell, Dandy Nichols
Play Dirty 🎬 Michael Caine, Nigel Davenport
A Touch of Love 🎬 Ian McKellen, Sandy Dennis
The Italian Job 🎬 Michael Caine, Benny Hill
Caine did not have a driver's license when he took on the film. He learned to drive while on-set (you never see him driving).

Mosquito Squadron 🎬 David McCallum, Suzanne Neve
Paint Your Wagon 🎬 Lee Marvin, Clint Eastwood
The Virgin Soldiers 🎬 Lynn Redgrave, Hywel Bennett
The Wild Bunch 🎬 William Holden, Ernest Borgnine
Easy Rider 🎬 Peter Fonda, Dennis Hopper
In the scene where Jack Nicholson tries marijuana for the first time and talks about UFOs, the actors really did get stoned.

The Gypsy Moths 🎬 Burt Lancaster, Deborah Kerr
Three Into Two Won't Go 🎬 Rod Steiger, Claire Bloom
Mackenna's Gold 🎬 Gregory Peck, Omar Sharif
Women in Love 🎬 Alan Bates, Oliver Reed
True Grit 🎬 John Wayne, Kim Darby
Despite being one of the most recognisable Western stars of all time, this is the only film for which Wayne won an Oscar.

Midnight Cowboy 🎬 Dustin Hoffman, Jon Voight
Voight told the studio he would do this film for nothing. They took that offer literally, only paying him $14 for his meals.

Kes 🎬 David Bradley, Lynne Perrie
Hannibal Brooks 🎬 Oliver Reed, Michael J Pollard
Battle of Britain 🎬 Christopher Plummer, Michael Caine
The Assassination Bureau 🎬 Oliver Reed, Diana Rigg
Age of Consent 🎬 James Mason, Helen Mirren
Cactus Flower 🎬 Walter Matthau, Ingrid Bergman
Oh! What a Lovely War 🎬 Laurence Olivier, John Gielgud
Hamlet 🎬 Nicol Williamson, Anthony Hopkins

Around the UK

A selection of national headlines from the year you turned 21. But how many can you remember?

- Ocean liner Queen Elizabeth 2 makes maiden voyage to New York
- British troops deployed in Northern Ireland in response to riots
- Death penalty for murder abolished
- Robin Knox-Johnston first to sail solo non-stop around globe
- Pre-decimal halfpenny coins phased out
- John Lennon weds Japanese artist Yoko Ono in Gibraltar
- Aussie media mogul Rupert Murdoch takes over News of the World
- Oarsman John Fairfax first to row solo across Atlantic
- Victoria Line opens on London Underground
- Charles, Prince of Wales, receives title in Caernarfon
- John Lennon returns MBE over UK complicity in Vietnam and Biafra
- Cult toy Space Hopper bounces into the shops
- The Beatles give last public performance on Apple Records roof
- Surreal sketch show Monty Python's Flying Circus airs on BBC1
- Ulster unionist Rev. Ian Paisley jailed over illegal protest
- Kray Twins Reggie and Ronnie sentenced to life for double murder
- Concorde makes first test flight at twice the speed of sound (right)
- Regular colour TV broadcasts begin on BBC1 and ITV
- Gibraltar's border with Spain closed by General Franco
- Lionel Bart's Dickensian musical Oliver! wins six Oscars
- Quirky kids' series The Clangers first broadcast on BBC1

Born this year:
- 12 Years A Slave director Steve McQueen born in London
- Award-winning actress Catherine Zeta-Jones born in Swansea
- Fashion designer Alexander McQueen born in London

Concorde made its first scheduled flight in 1976, but seven years earlier the first prototypes left the hangar: Concorde 001 (made in France), and Concorde 002, made in Bristol. Chief test pilot Brian Tubshaw (top left) is seen above preparing for its maiden flight on 9 April alongside co-pilot John Cochrane.

Concorde's livery changed several times over its lifetime but was only certified when predominantly white to keep the temperature down at supersonic speeds. There was one exception: in 1996, Pepsi paid to paint one aircraft blue as part of its $500m rebrand. The paint job carried a speed restriction.

The Biggest Hits When You Were 21

The artists you love at 21 are with you for life. How many of these hits from this milestone year can you still hum or sing in the bath?

Ob-La-Di, Ob-La-Da ♪ Marmalade
Ob-La-Di, Ob-La-Da was originally recorded by The Beatles and written by Paul McCartney – but not released in the UK or America. Its first live performance by any of The Beatles was in 2009.

Lily the Pink ♪ The Scaffold
Albatross ♪ Fleetwood Mac
Albatross – an instrumental – is the only Fleetwood Mac song to reach number one on the UK charts.

Blackberry Way ♪ The Move
Where Do You Go To ♪ Peter Sarstedt
Peter Sarstedt's elder brother Richard also had a number one hit in the UK with Well I Ask You in 1961 – performed under the moniker of Eden Kane.

I Heard It Through the Grapevine ♪ Marvin Gaye
Israelites ♪ Desmond Dekker & The Aces
Get Back ♪ The Beatles with Billy Preston
Dizzy ♪ Tommy Roe
Comedian Vic Reeves joined forces with the Wonder Stuff to release a cover of Dizzy in 1991. Both versions went to number one in the UK.

Honky Tonk Women ♪ The Rolling Stones
Je t'aime... moi non plus ♪ Jane Birkin
Sugar, Sugar ♪ The Archies

Popular Food in the 1960s

Convenient ready meals, 'fancy foreign food'… the sixties menu had it all. The chemists joined the dinner party, too, with additives and processes that made our new favourites easy and cheap to produce. We'd take a while to work out if this was always such a good idea!

Vesta curry or Chow Mein

Lager
'Lager' comes from the German word 'lagern', meaning 'to store', as lager takes longer to produce than other ales.

Coco Pops

Fish fingers
The largest fish finger ever made was 6ft long and weighed 136 kg. No word on whether the chef dipped it in ketchup.

Spaghetti Bolognese
You shouldn't include oregano, basil or garlic in the 'ragu' (not bolognese). And for goodness' sake, use tagliatelle, not spaghetti. Or… accept that it is as inauthentic as the Vesta curry and enjoy, like millions of Brits learned to do in the sixties.

Chicken Tikka Masala

Cheese and onion crisps
The first flavoured crisps were created by Joe 'Spud' Murphy (founder of Irish brand Taytos) in the late 1950s.

Crêpe Suzette

Chicken liver pâté

Angel Delight
Angel Delight doubled the dessert market when it was invented in 1967. Wallace and Gromit gave it another push in 1999.

Fray Bentos pies

Instant coffee

Frozen vegetables
Clarence Birdseye was the first person to freeze food for mass production, having got the idea from an Inuit in 1912.

Swedish meatballs

White bread
A new Chorleywood process introduced enzymes and additives and high-speed mixing. The result? Soft, cheap bread that sticks to the roof of your mouth. A nation couldn't get enough of it.

Fashion in the Sixties

However extravagant your taste in clothing, it's a dead cert that you could find something to shock and impress in the sixties. But whether you were old or bold enough to carry off a pair of bell bottoms or a paper dress is a secret that should remain between you and your photo albums!

Shift dresses
Mini skirt
Popularised by Mary Quant who named the skirt after her favourite car - although not everyone was a fan. Coco Chanel described the skirt as 'just awful', and it was banned in some European countries.

Five-point cut
Vidal Sassoon
Sassoon had a temper. He would give clients a slap of a comb if they touched their hair while he was cutting it.

John Bates
Biba
Biba started as a mail order business, advertising a pink gingham dress in the Daily Mirror. 17,000 orders were placed and a shop was opened. On its opening day, the store sold out of its only product line.

St Michael American Tan tights
Dr Scholl
Orlon, Crimplene, Terylene, Spandex, PVC and Vinyl
Paper dresses
Twiggy
Jackie Kennedy
In 1962, Jackie Kennedy wore a leopard print coat which caused a spike in demand for leopard skin, leading to the death of up to 250,000 leopards. The coat's designer, Oleg Cassini, felt guilty about it for the rest of his life.

Little black dress
First introduced by Coco Chanel in the 1920s, the little black dress received a fifties update from Christian Dior. Audrey Hepburn's LBD sold for £467,200 in 2006.

Jean Shrimpton
Jane Birkin

Around the World When You Turned 25

By your mid-twenties, TV coverage of news in far-flung places brought global stories into our homes almost as fast as they happened. How many do you remember?

- ✦ UK, Ireland and Denmark join European Economic Community
- ✦ Richard Nixon sworn in for second term as US president
- ✦ US legal case Roe vs Wade overturns state bans on abortion
- ✦ Joe Frazier loses boxing's heavyweight title to George Foreman
- ✦ Icelandic volcano Eldfell erupts for six months damaging 700 homes
- ✦ Chile's President Allende commits suicide during Pinochet coup
- ✦ Horror film The Exorcist terrifies US cinema audiences
- ✦ Egypt/Syria Yom Kippur attack triggers fourth Arab-Israeli war
- ✦ US troops leave Vietnam after Paris Peace Accord signed
- ✦ Spanish leader Carrero Blanco killed by ETA car bomb in Madrid
- ✦ Bahamas gain independence after 325 years of British rule
- ✦ US' first space station Skylab launches into Earth orbit
- ✦ Grandson of US oil tycoon J Paul Getty kidnapped in Rome
- ✦ Billie Jean King beats Bobby Riggs in US tennis' battle of sexes
- ✦ Televised hearings of Watergate case begin in US senate
- ✦ OPEC embargo against pro-Israel nations triggers oil crisis
- ✦ Australian architectural wonder Sydney Opera House opens
- ✦ Pink Floyd releases seminal album The Dark Side of The Moon
- ✦ 1.6 million UK workers strike over anti-inflation policy
- ✦ Ferdinand Marcos becomes Philippines' president for life

Born this year:
- ♪ Indian actress Aishwarya Rai born in Mangalore
- ♪ Google founder Larry Page born in Lansing, Michigan, USA
- ♪ Grand Slam tennis champ Monica Seles born in Novi Sad, Serbia
- ♪ US musician Pharrell Williams born in Virginia Beach, Virginia

Cars of the 1960s

For every much-loved Hillman Imp or trusted Vauxhall Victor, the sixties boasts a glamorous Aston Martin DB5 or a covetable Jaguar E-type. Has any decade delivered for the motoring public like the sixties?

Mini
Famously featured in the 1969 film The Italian Job, Mini manufacturer BMC didn't want the car used in the film and refused to donate any. However, the director insisted that British cars should be used in a British film and over a dozen were used.

Triumph Herald

Vauxhall Victor
The design of the Vauxhall Victor was based on the style of American cars, which didn't appeal to everyone's taste in 1960s Britain. The car also gained a negative reputation for rusting.

Austin 1100

Sunbeam Tiger

Aston Martin DB5
The Aston Martin DB5 has been described as the most famous car in the world, following its 1964 debut in Goldfinger. In 1968, the car used by James Bond in the film was stripped of the weapons and gadgets and resold as a used car. It was stolen in 1997 and is rumoured to be in the Middle East.

Hillman Hunter

Lotus Elan
The Lotus Elan was designed by Ron Hickman, who subsequently left Lotus and went on to design the Black & Decker Workmate. Early versions of the Elan were also available as a kit that could be assembled by the buyer.

Ford Cortina
The Ford Cortina was launched in 1962 and later proved to be the best-selling car of the 1970s in its Mk3 guise. Designed as a new version of the Ford Consul, the name was changed to Cortina after the Italian ski resort Cortina d'Ampezzo, host to the 1956 Winter Olympics.

Rover 3500

MGB

Vauxhall HA Viva

Books of the Decade

Were you a voracious bookworm in your twenties? Or a more reluctant reader, only drawn by the biggest titles of the day? Here are the new titles that fought for your attention.

1968	2001: A Space Odyssey by Arthur C Clarke
1969	Slaughterhouse-Five by Kurt Vonnegut
1969	Portnoy's Complaint by Philip Roth
1969	The Godfather by Mario Puzo
1969	The French Lieutenant's Woman by John Fowles
1969	Them by Joyce Carol Oates
1970	Deliverance by James Dickey
1971	An Accidental Man by Iris Murdoch
1971	The Day of the Jackal by Frederick Forsyth
1972	**Watership Down by Richard Adams** Watership Down was the first story Adams ever wrote, at the age of 52, based on tales he told his daughters in the car.
1973	Gravity's Rainbow by Thomas Pynchon
1973	Crash: A Novel by J G Ballard
1974	**Tinker, Tailor, Soldier, Spy by John le Carré** David Cornwell, the man behind the pseudonym John le Carré, drew on his personal experience working for MI5 and MI6. He appeared as an extra in the film of the book.
1974	**Carrie by Stephen King** Carrie was King's first novel, published when he was 26. He disliked the first draft and threw it in the bin; his wife found it and encouraged him to continue with the story.
1974	The Bottle Factory Outing by Beryl Bainbridge
1975	Shogun by James Clavell
1975	The Periodic Table by Primo Levi
1976	**Interview with the Vampire by Anne Rice** Rice wrote the novel following the death of her five-year-old daughter from leukaemia; the character of vampire child Claudia is inspired by her.
1977	Song of Solomon by Toni Morrison
1977	The Shining by Stephen King

Stamps in the Sixties

The UK hit its stride with commemorative stamps in the sixties. There were dry centenary and congress issues, but in 1965 the Postmaster General, Tony Benn, removed the need to include a large monarch portrait. The result? The kind of stamps every young collector would want.

1963	Freedom From Hunger
1963	Lifeboat Conference
1963	Red Cross Centenary Congress
1964	Opening of the Forth Road Bridge
1965	Winston Churchill Commemoration
1965	700th anniversary of Parliament
1965	Centenary of the Salvation Army
1965	**Antiseptic Surgery Centenary** Celebrates the introduction of surgical sterilisation by Joseph Lister.
1965	Commonwealth Arts Festival
1965	25th Anniversary of the Battle of Britain
1965	Opening of the Post Office Tower
1966	Westminster Abbey
1966	Landscapes
1966	**1966 World Cup** Stamps to mark England's role as hosts were hastily reissued in August 1966 with ENGLAND WINNERS added.
1966	British birds
1966	British technology
1966	900th anniversary of the Battle of Hastings
1966	**Christmas** The first UK Christmas stamps. The idea was championed by Tony Benn and the stamps designed by two 6-year-olds – winners of a Blue Peter competition.
1967	British wild flowers
1967	British paintings
1967	British discoveries and inventions
1967	Sir Francis Chichester's solo circumnavigation
1968	British bridges
1969	Concorde's first flight

Sixties TV Gameshows

Gameshows in the sixties were dominated by a few stalwarts, though a few short-lived experimental formats and US adaptions were tried. Without any serious competition, audiences were enormous. How many do you remember watching with your family?

Call My Bluff
Almost every episode from the first eight series of Call My Bluff has been wiped from the BBC archives. There were 263 episodes in series one to eight, and only seven episodes still survive.

Face the Music
Just a Minute
Ask the Family
University Challenge
Several celebrities appeared on University Challenge before they became famous. These include Stephen Fry, David Starkey, Sebastian Faulks, Julian Fellowes, and Miriam Margolyes (who swore when she answered a question incorrectly). University Challenge has a claim to be the longest running TV quiz show, alongside A Question of Sport.

For Love or Money
Mr and Mrs
After watching the Canadian version of Mr and Mrs, Derek Batey was inspired to develop a UK version of the show for Border Television. Batey hosted over 500 episodes, as well as 5,000 on stage after developing a theatrical version.

Play Your Hunch
Take Your Pick
Brain of Britain
Double Your Money
A November 1966 episode drew the nation's highest gameshow audience of nearly 20 million viewers.

Exit! It's the Way-Out Show
Many a Slip
Three Little Words
Crossword on 2

Around the UK

Another decade passes and you're well into adulthood. Were you reading the news, or making it? Here are the national stories that dominated the front pages.

✦ Bulgarian dissident killed by poisoned brolly tip at Waterloo
✦ Ian Botham sets cricketing test-match record for runs and wickets
✦ Hitchhiker's Guide to the Galaxy debuts on Radio 4
✦ Sex Pistols break up after disastrous US tour
✦ Charity Motability set up to provide cars for disabled people
✦ Strikes temporarily close down BBC and Times newspaper
✦ Prince Andrew joins Royal Navy
✦ Police introduce new radar gun to catch speeding motorists (right)
✦ Ford car workers strike over pensions and pay
✦ Anna Ford becomes ITN's first female newsreader
✦ Naomi James becomes first woman to sail solo around world
✦ State Earnings-Related Pension scheme introduced
✦ Pacific island nation Tuvalu gains independence from UK
✦ Protected species status ends otter hunting
✦ Concrete cows erected in Milton Keynes
✦ Regular live broadcasts of parliament begin on BBC radio
✦ Louise Brown becomes world's first IVF 'test-tube' baby
✦ Bakers' strike leads to panic-buying of bread
✦ Viv Anderson first black footballer to play for England
✦ New Liverpool Cathedral completed
✦ Wave of strikes hits UK during Winter of Discontent
✦ US soldier 'walks' across English Channel in 'water' shoes

Born this year:

⚭ Comic actor and TV host James Corden born in west London
⚭ England and Aston Villa striker Emile Heskey born in Leicester
⚭ Model and TV personality Katie Price born in Brighton

Lead poisoning has been known and observed for centuries but unleaded petrol didn't hit the forecourt until 1989 – and wasn't phased out globally until July 2021. This protester's particular cause was a lost one – the M25 was already opening in stages – but history is on her side.

With better roads come more opportunities to speed... until caught by new portable 'radar guns' which made their debut in 1978.

The Biggest Hits
When You Were 30

How many of these big tunes from the year you turned thirty will still strike a chord decades later?

Uptown Top Ranking 🎵 Althea and Donna
Figaro 🎵 Brotherhood of Man
Take a Chance on Me 🎵 ABBA
Wuthering Heights 🎵 Kate Bush
Kate Bush was only 18 years old when she wrote her timeless track, Wuthering Heights.

Lowry's Song 🎵 Brian and Michael
Night Fever 🎵 Bee Gees
Night Fever and a slew of other disco classics by the Bee Gees would form the soundtrack of the John Travolta movie, Saturday Night Fever.

Rivers of Babylon 🎵 Boney M
The lyrics to this disco classic are based on the Biblical Psalm 137:1-4 – which is about the Jewish people longing to return to their homeland.

Three Times a Lady 🎵 Commodores
Dreadlock Holiday 🎵 10cc
Co-writer of the song Graham Gouldman has never been to a cricket match – despite proclaiming his love for the song in the first chorus of this 70s anthem.

Rat Trap 🎵 The Boomtown Rats
Da Ya Think I'm Sexy? 🎵 Rod Stewart
Mary's Boy Child 🎵 Boney M

...and the Movies You Saw That Year, Too

From award winners to crowd pleasers, here are the movies that played as your third decade drew to a close.

The Boys from Brazil 🎟 Gregory Peck and Laurence Olivier
Warlords of Atlantis 🎟 Doug McClure, Peter Gilmore
The Stud 🎟 Joan Collins and Oliver Tobias
Convoy 🎟 Kris Kristofferson, Ali MacGraw
Force 10 from Navarone 🎟 Robert Shaw, Harrison Ford
Grease 🎟 John Travolta, Olivia Newton-John
Sandy's 'bad girl' outfit at the end of the movie was so tight, Newton-John had to be sewn into the pants every morning.

Coma 🎟 Geneviève Bujold, Michael Douglas
Days of Heaven 🎟 Richard Gere, Brooke Adams
The Medusa Touch 🎟 Richard Burton, Lino Ventura
The Lord of the Rings 🎟 John Hurt, Christopher Guard
The Wild Geese 🎟 Richard Burton, Roger Moore
The Deer Hunter 🎟 Robert De Niro, Christopher Walken
The Deer Hunter proved to be the final film of John Cazale, who was dying of bone cancer during production.

The Thirty Nine Steps 🎟 Robert Powell, David Warner
The Shout 🎟 Alan Bates, John Hurt
Coming Home 🎟 Jane Fonda, Jon Voight
Watership Down 🎟 John Hurt, Richard Briers
Death on the Nile 🎟 Peter Ustinov, Lois Chiles
California Suite 🎟 Jane Fonda, Alan Alda
Heaven Can Wait 🎟 Warren Beatty, James Mason
Halloween 🎟 Jamie Lee Curtis, Donald Pleasence
Jamie Lee Curtis's film debut. She was so disappointed in her performance she thought she would be fired on the first day.

Midnight Express 🎟 Brad Davis, Irene Miracle
Superman 🎟 Christopher Reeve, Gene Hackman
Director Richard Donner promised to shave his own moustache if Hackman did the same for his role as Lex Luthor. Once the actor shaved, Donner revealed he was wearing a fake moustache.

Animal House 🎟 John Belushi, Peter Riegert

Around the House

Sometimes with a fanfare but often by stealth, inventions and innovations transformed the 20th-century household. Here's what arrived between the ages of 10 and 30.

1958	Pledge furniture polish
1959	The dimmer switch
1961	Cordless power drills
1962	**Satellite television**

Satellite television
Despite being invented in 1962, satellite television did not reach the UK until 1990 when British Satellite Broadcasting was launched, merging with Sky to become BSkyB.

1963	Push button telephones
1963	Lava lamps
1964	Flat screen and Portable TVs
1965	**AstroTurf**

AstroTurf
AstroTurf was originally called ChemGrass, and invented by chemicals giant Monsanto. It was rebranded in 1966.

1965	Cordless phones
1965	Plastic chairs
1967	Ariel detergent
1967	**The Blow Chair**

The Blow Chair
The Blow Chair was the first mass-produced inflatable chair. The Blow Chair represents one of the Anti-Design movement's core beliefs that objects should be temporary.

1969	Bean bags
1969	Comfort fabric softener
1970	**Blu-Tack**

Blu-Tack
The largest Blu-Tack sculpture is a 2007 creation called Spider Biggus. it uses 4,000 packs of the blue stuff.

1971	Garden strimmers
1972	Scientific calculators
1973	BIC lighter
1974	Sticky notes
1975	Betamax movies
1976	**VHS movies**

VHS movies
The last film ever released on VHS was David Cronenberg's 2006 thriller, A History of Violence.

British Prime Ministers in Your Lifetime

These are the occupants of 10 Downing Street, London, during your lifetime, not including Larry the resident cat. Don't be deceived by that unassuming, black, blast-proof door: Number 10 features a warren of more than 100 rooms.

1945–51	Clement Attlee
1951–55	Sir Winston Churchill
1955–57	Sir Anthony Eden
1957–63	**Harold Macmillan** Macmillan was the scion of a wealthy publishing family, but the biggest secret of his life was kept under wraps: his wife Dorothy's 30-year affair with fellow Conservative (and Krays associate) Robert Boothby. Macmillan died aged 92; his last words were, 'I think I will go to sleep now.'
1963–64	Sir Alec Douglas-Home
1964–70	Harold Wilson
1970–74	Edward Heath
1974–76	Harold Wilson
1976–79	James Callaghan
1979–90	**Margaret Thatcher** 'Today we were unlucky,' said the chilling statement from the IRA, 'but remember we only have to be lucky once.' The 1994 bombing of the Grand hotel in Brighton killed five; others were left with lifelong injuries.
1990–97	John Major
1997–2007	Tony Blair
2007–10	Gordon Brown
2010–16	David Cameron
2016–19	**Theresa May** Asked in a pre-election interview about the naughtiest thing she'd ever done, May said that she'd run through a field of wheat, and that the farmers 'weren't too happy'.
2019–22	Boris Johnson
2022	Liz Truss
2022–	Rishi Sunak

Household Goods in 1962

The basket of 1962 is beginning to look like the basket of today. Alongside new convenient foods there's a fresh emphasis on looking smart inside and outside the home.

Sliced white bread

Chocolate coated biscuits

Dry cleaning

Potato crisps

Crisps entered the basket of goods in 1962, the same year Golden Wonder (bought by Imperial Tobacco) launched cheese and onion flavoured crisps. Golden Wonder, Smith's and soon Walkers fought for the market, and consumption rocketed.

Oven ready chicken

Cuts of halibut

Second-hand car

Welfare milk scheme

Ground coffee

Frozen croquettes

As more homes had freezers and the desire for ready meals increased, frozen food was all the rage. Frozen croquettes were released in the early 1960s and were a resounding success.

Canned fruit salad

Canned fruit salad was designed to use the fruit scraps that couldn't be used in canning. Fruit salad arrived in the 1940s and became one of the most popular canned fruits available. You could even use it to make a fruit salad cake.

TV set rental

Gloss paint

Ceiling paper

Jeans

Latex backed carpet

Refrigerator

Ready-made suit

Terylene slacks

Created in Manchester in 1941, Terylene revolutionised clothing in the 1950s. It was used by Mary Quant to make the original miniskirts, and Ray Davies of The Kinks advertised it.

Around the World When You Turned 35

It's a big news day every day, somewhere in the world. Here are the stories that the media thought you'd want to read in the year of your 35th birthday.

+ 'Butcher of Lyon' Klaus Barbie tried for war crimes in France
+ US engineer Chuck Hull invents 3D printing
+ Over 180 Ash Wednesday bushfires devastate South Australia
+ 106 million watch last episode of Korean war series M*A*S*H
+ Unmanned spacecraft Pioneer 10 is first to leave our solar system
+ Mystery fainting illness affects Arab teens on Israel's West Bank
+ Australian helicopter pilot first to fly solo around the world
+ Lowest ever Earth temperature -89.2°C recorded in Antarctica
+ Drought causes widespread famine in Ethiopia, with millions dying
+ Korean airliner shot down over Soviet airspace, killing 269
+ Hitler diaries found by German magazine Stern prove fake
+ Turkish Republic of Northern Cyprus declared
+ First US woman in space Sally Ride blasts off on NASA Challenger
+ US man with 105 wives goes on trial for bigamy and fraud
+ Word-processing program Microsoft Word released
+ Suicide bomb attack on the US Embassy in Beirut kills 63
+ Biopic Gandhi wins eight Oscars including Best Picture
+ US troops invade Grenada to prevent communist takeover
+ Marcos opponent Benigno Aquino shot dead in Philippines

Born this year:
+ Tennis player Kim Clijsters born in Bilzen, Belgium
+ Thor actor Chris Hemsworth born in Melbourne, Australia
+ US actress Mila Kunis born in Chernivtsi, Ukraine

Beer of the Seventies

You could haul a seven-pint tin of Watneys Party Seven to a celebration. Someone would be drinking bland Watneys Red, or Courage Tavern ('It's what your right arm's for'). But how about a drop of that cold, refreshing lager you tried on holiday? 'Mine's a pint!' said millions of Brits.

Watneys Party Seven
Whitbread Tankard
Watneys Red
Double Diamond

Carlsberg
The inventor of Carlsberg, JC Jacobsen, gave a Ted Talk on his life philosophy in 2017 – 130 years after he died. He was brought back to life via hologram and even fielded questions from the audience.

Heineken
The Heineken International company owns more than 250 other brands, many of which you'll probably recognise such as Amstel, Desperados and Strongbow.

Tennant's Gold Label

Guinness
When Arthur Guinness started his now-famous business he rented an unused brewery on a 9,000-year lease – though the contract was eventually voided when the company bought the land and surrounding areas to expand the business.

Worthington E
Carling Black Label
Harp
Stella Artois
Ind Coope Super
Younger's Scotch Ale
Bass Charrington

Strongbow
HP Bulmer named his drink after one of the greatest knights in English history, Richard de Clare, who was given the nickname Strongbow.

Long Life

Seventies TV Gameshows

With light entertainment increasingly becoming the bedrock of TV channel success, the seventies saw an explosion of formats from gimmicks to US imports. Which ones got you shouting at the telly?

It's a Knockout
Although this show began in 1966 and it limped on into the new century, the seventies was It's a Knockout's golden age, thanks in no small part to presenter Stuart Hall. The winning teams proceeded to represent the UK at the European final, Jeux Sans Frontières.

I'm Sorry I Haven't a Clue

Jokers Wild

My Music

A Question of Sport
A Question of Sport is the world's longest running TV sports quiz. The first episode was recorded in 1970 in a converted chapel in Rusholme, Manchester, and the show is still recorded in the city as it surpasses 1,300 episodes.

Quote... Unquote

Whodunnit?

Mastermind

Screen Test

Celebrity Squares
Inspired by the game noughts and crosses, Celebrity Squares was based on the US gameshow Hollywood Squares. The original run was presented by Bob Monkhouse, who also returned to host the revival of the show in the 1990s.

Gambit

The Generation Game

The Golden Shot

The Indoor League

Password

Runaround

Sale of the Century

The Sky's the Limit

Winner Takes All

Popular Boys' Names

Just as middle age crept up unnoticed, so the most popular names also evolved. The traditional choices – possibly including yours – were fast losing their appeal to new parents.

Christopher
Christopher takes a ten-year stint at the top, replacing Paul but ultimately unable to keep Thomas at bay.

James
David
Daniel
Michael
Matthew
Andrew
Richard
Paul
Mark
Thomas
Adam
Robert
John
Lee
Benjamin
Steven
Jonathan
Craig
Stephen
Simon
Nicholas
Peter
Anthony
Alexander
Gary
Ian

Rising and falling stars:
The rapid turnover in fashion hasn't abated: again, a third of names in this list won't be seen again, from Barry to Brian, Antony to Abdul.

Popular Girls' Names

It's a similar story for girls' names. Increasing numbers took their infant inspiration from popular culture. The worlds of music, film and now the internet are all fertile hunting grounds for those in need of inspiration.

Sarah

Laura

Gemma

Never seen in the Top 100 before, here's Gemma riding high as the third most popular name in the UK.

Emma

Rebecca

Claire

Victoria

Samantha

Rachel

Amy

Jennifer

Nicola

Katie

Lisa

Kelly

Natalie

Louise

Michelle

Hayley

Hannah

Helen

Charlotte

Joanne

Lucy

Elizabeth

Leanne

Danielle

Rising and falling stars:

This Top 100 list spans much of the eighties and sees a one-off appearance of Charlene. In not-unrelated news, nearly 20 million people watched Jason marry Kylie on Neighbours...

F1 Champions

If you fancy your chances in Formula One, start young. Sebastian Vettel won at 23. *El Maestro*, Juan Manuel Fangio, is the oldest winner to date, at 46. The field is wide open for an older champ, right?

Jackie Stewart 🏆 (1969,71,73)

Jochen Rindt 🏆 (1970)

Rindt was awarded the Drivers' Championship posthumously after crashing at Monza, having built an unassailable season lead. A poorly-fitted crash barrier was the main cause of death. He was the third F1 driver to die that year.

Emerson Fittipaldi 🏆 (1972,74)

Niki Lauda 🏆 (1975,77,84)

Niki Lauda was also an aviation entrepreneur, founding three airlines in Austria. He also held a commercial pilot's licence.

James Hunt 🏆 (1976)

Mario Andretti 🏆 (1978)

Jody Scheckter 🏆 (1979)

Alan Jones 🏆 (1980)

Nelson Piquet 🏆 (1981,83,87)

Nelson Piquet lost his civilian driving licence in 2007 due to numerous speeding and parking offences. He was ordered to attend a week of lessons and pass an exam.

Keke Rosberg 🏆 (1982)

Alain Prost 🏆 (1985-6,89,93)

Ayrton Senna 🏆 (1988,90-1)

Two days before Senna's fatal crash at Imola, he was early to the scene of a near-fatal crash for Rubens Barrichello. One day before, he inspected the car of Roland Ratzenberger as the mortally-injured Austrian was taken to hospital – the same facility that would attempt to save Senna's life the following day after his crash on the same corner. An Austrian flag was later found in Senna's cockpit, intended to be unfurled as a tribute to Ratzenberger.

Nigel Mansell 🏆 (1992)

Michael Schumacher 🏆 (1994-5,2000-04)

Michael Schumacher was one of a handful of drivers to appear as themselves in the Pixar film Cars, voicing a Ferrari F430.

Fashion in the Seventies

The decade that taste forgot? Or a kickback against the sixties and an explosion of individuality? Skirts got shorter (and longer). Block colours and peasant chic vied with sequins and disco glamour. How many of your seventies outfits would you still wear today?

Flares
Platform shoes
Laura Ashley
While working as a secretary, Laura Ashley was inspired to produce printed fabric after seeing a display at the Victoria and Albert Museum. Struggling to make a profit, Laura Ashley and her husband and children once lived in tents in Wales for six months.

Gucci
Diane Von Furstenberg
Tie Dye
Kaftans
Brought to western culture via the hippie trail, the kaftan's popularity was boosted further when Elizabeth Taylor wore a kaftan-inspired dress for her second wedding to Richard Burton in 1975.

Liza Minnelli
Lurex and suede
David Bowie
Afro, braids or a perm
Jumpsuit
Sequin hot pants
Moon boots
Double denim
Double denim garnered the nickname the 'Canadian tuxedo' after Bing Crosby was refused entry to a hotel in Vancouver because he wore a denim ensemble. Levi subsequently designed Crosby a denim tuxedo.

Vivienne Westwood
Previously a primary school teacher, Vivienne Westwood lived in an ex-council flat in Clapham until 2000. Her son from her relationship with Malcolm McLaren founded lingerie brand Agent Provocateur.

Household Goods in 1970

Frozen foods and eating out swallow up an increasingly larger share of the family budget in the seventies. Or how about a day trip (don't forget your AA membership and your mac), then home for a sweet sherry?

Frozen chicken

Mushrooms

Frozen beans

Sherry

Sherry consumption peaked in the UK in the 1970s following the development of sweet versions – often using added syrups or sugars – known as creams and developed for British palates.

Night storage heater

Plastic Mackintosh

MOT test

Introduced in 1960, the MOT was designed to test the brakes, lights, and steering of all vehicles over 10 years old. This was progressively reduced to every three years by 1967, and the test changed to include tyres.

State school meal

Canteen meal

Cup of tea

The 1970s saw a significant increase in eating out, so a cup of tea was added to the basket. Despite Britain's reputation as tea lovers, coffee sales overtook tea sales for the first time in 1986.

Cafe sandwich

Local authority rent

Local authority rent was added to the basket of goods in the 1970s; by 1979, 42% of Britons lived in council homes.

Paper handkerchiefs

Auto association subs

Keg of ale

Fresh cream

Gammon

While gammon gained popularity during the 1970s due to its unlikely pairing with pineapple rings, the word 'gammon' is now also used as an insult towards the political right, coined in response to 'snowflake'.

Post-war Chocolate

You'll find nearly all of these on the supermarket shelves, even though the most recently invented chocolate bar here was brought to market thirty years ago. Gulp.

1948	Fudge
1951	**Bounty** If you wanted to sell a chocolate bar with curved ends and swirls on the top, in theory there's nothing that maker Mars could do to stop you: the shape was decreed not distinctive enough to trademark in 2009. Do check with a lawyer first, though.
1957	Munchies
1958	Picnic
1962	**After Eight Mint Chocolate Thins** A billion of these are churned out every year (although we've never heard anyone call them chocolate thins).
1962	Topic
1963	Toffee Crisp
1967	Twix
1970	Chomp
1970	Curly Wurly
1973	Freddo
1976	**Double Decker** Double Deckers contain raisins, don't they? Not any more: they were removed from the recipe during the eighties.
1976	Starbar
1976	**Yorkie** 'It's not for girls,' said the adverts. The sexist marketing of Yorkie reached its peak – or trough – in 2005 with special pink editions. By 2011 the complaints outweighed the commercial advantage. The 'men only' angle was dropped.
1978	Lion Bar
1980	Drifter
1983	**Wispa** For twenty years, Wispa was the go-to Aero alternative. But then in 2003 it was gone. A predictable outcry followed and in 2007 it was back on the shelves. Phew.
992	Time Out

Books of the Decade

Family, friends, TV, and more: there are as many midlife distractions as there are books on the shelf. Did you get drawn in by these bestsellers, all published in your thirties?

1978	The Sea, The Sea by Iris Murdoch
1978	Tales of the City by Armistead Maupin
1979	**The Hitchhiker's Guide to the Galaxy by Douglas Adams** If 42 is the meaning of life, what's the meaning of 42? Nothing. Adams said it was simply a random number he chose. There's a message in there somewhere...
1979	A Bend in the River by V S Naipaul
1979	Sophie's Choice by William Styron
1980	A Confederacy of Dunces by John Kennedy Toole
1980	The Name of the Rose by Umberto Eco
1981	Midnight's Children by Salman Rushdie
1982	The Color Purple by Alice Walker
1982	**Schindler's Ark by Thomas Keneally** Keneally wrote Schindler's Ark - later retitled Schindler's List - after he met Holocaust survivor Leopold Page. Schindler is credited with saving over 1,000 lives. He is the only former Nazi to be buried on Jerusalem's Mount Zion.
1983	The Colour of Magic by Terry Pratchett
1983	Waterland by Graham Swift
1984	Money by Martin Amis
1984	The Wasp Factory by Iain Banks
1985	**The Handmaid's Tale by Margaret Atwood** The Communist reign of Nicolae Ceaușescu in Romania partially inspired Atwood to write The Handmaid's Tale. While he was in power, women had to have four babies; abortions were illegal, contraception was banned, and women were examined for signs of pregnancy at work.
1985	Blood Meridian by Cormac McCarthy
1985	Perfume by Patrick Suskind
1986	The Old Devils by Kingsley Amis
1986	It by Stephen King
1987	Beloved by Toni Morrison

Around the World When You Turned 40

Which of these international news events were on your radar as you clocked up four decades on the planet?

✦ Australia celebrates bicentenary of its founding
✦ Israeli commandos kill PLO deputy leader Abu Jihad in Tunisia
✦ First World AIDS Day held to raise awareness of HIV
✦ Francois Mitterand re-elected as President of France
✦ Soviet troops start to withdraw from Afghanistan
✦ Train collision at Paris Gare de Lyon kills 56
✦ Estonians hold mass singing protests against Soviet occupation
✦ Osama bin Laden forms Islamist terrorist group Al-Qaeda
✦ UN-brokered ceasefire ends eight-year Iran-Iraq war
✦ Fires in US Yellowstone National Park scorch millions of acres
✦ Canadian runner Ben Johnson fails drug test at Seoul Olympics
✦ World's first Fairtrade label Max Havelaar set up in Netherlands
✦ Burmese military cracks down on pro-democracy protests
✦ Spitak earthquake in Armenia kills over 25,000
✦ 290 die as US warship accidentally fires on Iranian airliner
✦ NASA scientist advises manmade global warming has begun
✦ US author Toni Morrison wins Pulitzer Prize for novel Beloved
✦ Pakistan's Benazir Bhutto is first woman to head up Islamic state

Born this year:
⚬ Canadian actor Michael Cera born in Brampton, Ontario
⚬ Pop star Robyn Rihanna Fenty born in St Michael, Barbados
⚬ German tennis player Angelique Kerber born in Bremen

Around the UK

Here are the headline stories from across the country in the year you hit 40.

+ Fire on North Sea oil rig Piper Alpha leaves 167 dead
+ Bomb explodes on Pan Am flight over Lockerbie, killing 270
+ Prince Charles avoids Swiss avalanche that kills close friend
+ Loyalists attack IRA funerals at Belfast cemetery
+ 35 dead in Clapham Junction triple-train collision
+ 80,000 honour Nelson Mandela at Wembley Stadium concert (right)
+ Government bans broadcasts of interviews with IRA members
+ SAS officers kill three IRA suspects in Gibraltar
+ Nurses strike in protest over pay and NHS funding
+ Art gallery Tate Liverpool opens
+ New pub laws allow all-day opening in England and Wales
+ Gay rights activists invade BBC News studio
+ Health minister Edwina Curry resigns over egg salmonella scare
+ First killer caught using DNA evidence
+ Dog license scrapped
+ Golfer Sandy Lyle becomes first Briton to win US Masters
+ Celebrity news magazine Hello! first published in UK
+ First BBC Red Nose Day raises £15m for charity
+ Pound note removed from circulation, replaced with £1 coin
+ Seamen at British ports defy union calls to return to work
+ Paddy Ashdown heads new Social and Liberal Democratic Party

Born this year:
- World heavyweight champion boxer Tyson Fury born in Manchester
- Singer-songwriter Adele (Adkins) born in Tottenham, London
- Rapper Tinie Tempah born Patrick Chukwuemeka Okogwu in London

The Nelson Mandela Freedom March used the opportunity of Mandela's 70th birthday to call for his release on a journey from Glasgow to London. Just twenty-five marchers took part each day, one for each year spent in prison by Mandela. The march culminated at the Nelson Mandela Birthday Tribute at a packed Wembley stadium; 600 million more watched the event worldwide. Despite the resistance of the UK and US governments, Nelson Mandela – and his cause – were now the talk of households worldwide.

The Biggest Hits When You Were 40

Big tunes for a big birthday: how many of them enticed your middle-aged party guests onto the dance floor?

Heaven Is a Place on Earth ♪ Belinda Carlisle
I Think We're Alone Now ♪ Tiffany
I Should Be So Lucky ♪ Kylie Minogue
Kylie's first seven singles all peaked in the top two spots on the UK Singles Chart. I Should Be So Lucky went straight to number one.

Heart ♪ Pet Shop Boys
Perfect ♪ Fairground Attraction
She's Leaving Home ♪ Billy Bragg
Doctorin' the Tardis ♪ The Timelords
I Owe You Nothing ♪ Bros
Bros became the unwitting comedy stars of their unintentionally gripping 2018 documentary Bros: After the Screaming Stops in which the pair deconstruct their sometimes fractious relationship.

A Groovy Kind of Love ♪ Phil Collins
A 1965 hit, covered by Collins and used for Buster, the film starring Collins about the Great Train Robbery. Charles and Diana cancelled their attendance at the première to avoid appearing to condone 'violence as entertainment'.

Desire ♪ U2
One Moment in Time ♪ Whitney Houston
Orinoco Flow ♪ Enya
Enya is one of the world's best-selling artists. She writes all songs in Irish originally, and has sung in ten languages. She doesn't tour and lives in a well-defended castle.

First Time ♪ Robin Beck

Popular Food in the 1970s

Roll out the hostess trolley, seventies food is ready to be served. If it's not highly processed, artificially coloured, moulded and served in a novelty dish, is it even food? Still, most of it went down very well with the kids – and still does today, given half a chance.

Lemon meringue pie
Cheese and pineapple
Black Forest Gâteau
The Black Forest Gâteau is named after the kirsch alcohol made from Black Forest sour cherries, rather than the Black Forest region in Germany.

Dream Topping
Mateus Rose, Liebfraumilch and Chianti
Cornetto
Cornetto cones were created by Spica, an Italian ice-cream company, in 1976. The company was bought by Unilever not long after, who then marketed the dessert in Europe.

Quavers
Quiche
Unlike the gâteau above, quiche Lorraine *was* named after the area in which it was created. It is considered a French dish, even though Lorraine was under German rule at the time.

Pot Noodle
The original Pot Noodle made in 1979 did not contain a sauce sachet – these were only added in 1992.

Fondue
Smash
Scampi in a basket
Banoffee pie
Chili con carne
Chili is the state dish of Texas, where many people think the recipe originated. Before WWII, hundreds of individual parlours all insisted they had their own secret recipe.

Prawn cocktails
Profiteroles
The Full English Breakfast

Cars of the 1970s

How did you get around in the seventies? Was it in one of the decade's fancy new Range Rovers, or perhaps something more modest like a Morris Marina? Here are the decade's most famous (and infamous) cars.

Ford Capri

Vauxhall HC Viva

Ford Escort

Introduced in 1968, the Ford Escort went on to be the best-selling car in Britain in the 1980s and 1990s. The car was brought back into the spotlight in 2013, when it was featured in Fast & Furious 6.

Jaguar XJ

Triumph TR7

Austin Allegro

Austin Maxi

The Austin Maxi was the first British five-door hatchback, and one of the first cars to be featured on the BBC's Wheelbase show.

Ford Cortina

Ford Granada

Designed as a European executive car, the Granada was popular for taxi and police car use. It was also modified for use as a hearse and limousine, and was often seen in The Sweeney.

Leyland Princess

Triumph Dolomite

Vauxhall Cavalier

Range Rover

Morris Marina

The popular Morris Marina is ranked amongst the worst cars ever built. The car was released with poor suspension, chronic understeer, and windscreen wipers fitted the wrong way round.

Hillman Avenger

Saab 99

Datsun Sunny

BMW 316

Volkswagen Beetle

Affectionately known as the bug in English-speaking countries, it is called turtle in Bolivia, frog in Indonesia, and hunchback in Poland.

Household Goods in 1980

Mortgage interest rates were around 15% as we went into the eighties, not much lower as we left, and added to our basket in 1980. If you had any money left over perhaps you were spending it on home perms, cement and lamb's liver!

Lamb's liver

Tea bags
Tea is one of the few items included in the basket since the start. Tea bags were added in 1980; loose tea was removed in 2002.

Smash
Smash sales soared following the 1974 TV adverts featuring the Smash Martians. It was replaced in 1987 by oven chips.

Cider

Wine

Mortgage Interest

White spirit

Cement

Toilet seat

Electric plug

Colour TV
Colour TV sets outnumbered black and white sets in 1976.

Record player

Cassette recorder
Cassette recorders were first introduced by Philips in the 1960s and were originally intended for dictation and journalists.

Electric hairdryer

Carpet sweeper

Continental quilt

Drycell batteries

Colour photo film

Briefcase

Home perm

National Trust fees
Membership to the National Trust significantly increased throughout the 1980s (around 5.6 million people are members today). The Giant's Causeway is the most visited national attraction.

Olympic Medallists in Your Life

With seven gold medals, Jason Kenny is without equal while the unique achievements of Laura Trott – now Mrs Kenny – brings the household tally to twelve. Meanwhile, over at the Paralympics, swimmer-cyclist Sarah Storey has an incredible 17 gold medals. And medals of all colours? Here are the heroes of Team GB at the Summer Olympics.

Jason Kenny (9) ⚭ Cycling

Bradley Wiggins (8) ⚭ Cycling
Britain's most decorated Olympian until Kenny took the crown in Tokyo, Wiggo acquired various nicknames throughout his career. In France he was referred to as 'Le Gentleman', while the Dutch apparently called him 'The Banana with the Sideburns'.

Chris Hoy (7) ⚭ Cycling

Laura Kenny (6) ⚭ Cycling
Our most successful female Olympian with five gold medals, Trott (now Kenny) began life with a collapsed lung and asthma.

Steve Redgrave (6) ⚭ Rowing

Max Whitlock (6) ⚭ Gymnastics

Charlotte Dujardin (6) ⚭ Equestrianism

Ben Ainslie (5) ⚭ Sailing
Known for his hot temper, Ben Ainslie has accused competitors of teaming up against him. He was disqualified from the world championships in Australia for confronting a photographer who Ainslie felt had impeded his progress.

Adam Peaty (5) ⚭ Swimming

Katherine Grainger (5) ⚭ Rowing
Grainger is the first British woman to win medals at five successive Olympic games, from Sydney to Rio.

Mo Farah (4) ⚭ Athletics

Matthew Pinsent (4) ⚭ Rowing

Ed Clancy (4) ⚭ Cycling

Ian Stark (4) ⚭ Equestrianism

Louis Smith (4) ⚭ Gymnastics

Becky Adlington (4) ⚭ Swimming

Seb Coe (4) ⚭ Athletics

Ginny Leng (4) ⚭ Equestrianism

It's striking that our most decorated Olympians did so in recent decades. Of the 18 athletes earning four medals or more since you were born, Seb Coe came off the starting blocks first: he won his first medal at the 1980 Moscow Olympics at the age of 23 (shortly after breaking the 1,000 metre record in Oslo, above).

Run the slide rule over every modern Olympics, starting in 1896, and only six more GB athletes have achieved the same phenomenal success.

Winter Olympics Venues Since You Were Born

Unless you're an athlete or winter sports fan, the Winter Olympics can slip past almost unnoticed. These are the venues; can you remember the host countries and years?

Lillehammer
Cortina d'Ampezzo
Oslo
Salt Lake City
Sapporo
Albertville
The last Games to be held in the same year as the Summer Olympics, with the next Winter Olympics held two years later.

Turin
Grenoble
Beijing
Sarajevo
Lake Placid
Sochi
Innsbruck (twice)
This usually snowy city experienced its mildest winter in 60 years; the army transported snow and ice from the mountains. Nevertheless, twelve years later, the Winter Olympics were back.

Squaw Valley
Nagano
St Moritz
The first Winter Olympics to be held for 12 years and named the 'Games of Renewal'; Japan and Germany were not invited.

Calgary
Vancouver
PyeongChang

Answers: Lillehammer: Norway, 1994; Cortina d'Ampezzo: Italy, 1956; Oslo: Norway, 1952; Salt Lake City: USA, 2002; Sapporo: Japan, 1972; Albertville: France, 1992; Turin: Italy, 2006; Grenoble: France, 1968; Beijing: China, 2022; Sarajevo: Yugoslavia, 1984; Lake Placid: USA, 1980; Sochi: Russia, 2014; Innsbruck: Austria, 1964; Squaw Valley: USA, 1960; Nagano: Japan, 1998; St Moritz: Switzerland, 1948; Calgary: Canada, 1988; Innsbruck: Austria, 1976; Vancouver: Canada, 2010; PyeongChang: South Korea, 2018

Fashion in the Eighties

Eighties fashion was many things, but subtle wasn't one of them. Brash influences were everywhere from aerobics to Wall Street, from pop princesses to preppy polo shirts. The result was chaotic, but fun. How many eighties throwbacks still lurk in your closet?

Shoulder pads or puffed sleeves

Scrunchies
Patented in 1987 by nightclub singer Rommy Revson, the first scrunchie was designed using the waistband of her pyjama bottoms. The softer alternative to hair bands was named after Revson's dog Scunchie (no, that's not a typo).

Conical bras
Inspired by 1950s bullet bras, Jean Paul Gaultier introduced the cone bra in 1984. As a child he fashioned the bra for his teddy bear; years later he reworked the look for Madonna's Blonde Ambition tour in 1990.

Acid wash jeans

Slogan t-shirts
Designer Katharine Hamnett introduced slogan t-shirts, famously revealing one displaying an anti-nuclear statement when meeting Margaret Thatcher in 1984. Wham opted for 'Choose Life'; for Frankie Goes to Hollywood it was 'Frankie Says Relax'.

Leotards and leg-warmers
Leg-warmers reached the masses following the release of Fame and Flashdance, as well as Jane Fonda exercise videos. Nowadays, leg-warmers are even worn by babies while they have their nappies changed.

Deely boppers, bangle earrings or a polka dot hair bow
Pedal pushers or leggings
Guyliner
Levi 501s
Pixie boots
Ra-ra skirt and PVC belts

Dr Martens
Dr Martens were designed by a German soldier to aid the recovery of his broken foot. Pete Townshend of The Who was the first rock star to wear the boots on stage, and the shoe was adopted by numerous subcultures.

World Buildings

Buildings that are known the world over for all the right (and the wrong) reasons and were opened before you turned 40.

1955	**Hiroshima Peace Museum, Hiroshima** Built following the atomic bombing of Hiroshima as an enduring symbol of peace and to educate, the museum receives over a million visitors each year.
1958	Tokyo Tower, Tokyo
1958	Expo '58 World's Fair, Brussels
1958	Seagram Building, New York
1959	**The Guggenheim, New York** Architect Frank Lloyd Wright produced over 700 sketches of the museum. Upon opening, Woody Allen commented that it looked like a giant lavatory basin.
1961	**Space Needle, Seattle** Built for the 1962 World's Fair. Early shape designs included a tethered balloon and a cocktail shaker before the iconic final design was chosen.
1968	Madison Square Garden, New York City, New York
1969	John Hancock Center, Chicago
1973	Sears Tower, Chicago, Illinois
1973	World Trade Center, New York
1973	**Sydney Opera House, Sydney** The estimated cost for the construction was AU$7m (£4m). It ended up costing AU$102m (£59m), and took 14 years to build rather than the four years planned.
1976	CN Tower, Toronto
1977	Pompidou Centre, Paris
1981	Sydney Tower, Sydney
1990	Washington National Cathedral, Washington DC
1983	**Trump Tower, New York** How many floors there are in Trump Tower? An easy question, right? It was built with 58 floors. But Trump wasn't happy… the ceilings are high on some floors, so the numbers jump from the 6th to the 13th floor. Now it has 68!

Grand Designs

Governments around the world spent much of the 20th century nation building (and rebuilding). Here is a selection of striking civil engineering achievements between the ages of 0 and 30.

1955	Disneyland Castle, Anaheim, California
1955	Battersea Power Station, London
1959	**M1 Motorway, London & Leeds** The M1 was the second motorway built in the UK, and it was the first motorway to join two cities. The first section opened in 1959, and the most recent section was added in 1999.
1959	Kariba Dam, Kariba
1962	Butlins, Minehead
1965	Mont Blanc Tunnel, France & Italy
1965	Zeeland Bridge, Netherlands
1966	**Almondsbury Interchange, Bristol & Gloucester** The Almondsbury Interchange was the first example of a four-level stack in the UK, and remains one of only three of its kind in the country.
1967	**Second Blackwall Tunnel, London** The second Blackwall tunnel is relatively straight, unlike the first which is curved. That was to avoid a sewer, but also reportedly so that horses (the main means of transport when built) didn't see daylight at the other end and bolt.
1969	Humber Refinery, Northern Lincolnshire
1970	Aswan Dam, Aswan
1970	Hyde Park Barracks, London
1971	**Spaghetti Junction, Birmingham** Officially the Gravelly Hill Interchange, Spaghetti Junction was named by the Guinness Book of World Records as 'the most complex interchange on the British road system'.
1973	Bosphorus Bridge, Istanbul
1976	**Sonnenberg Tunnel, Lucerne** A 5,000 ft road tunnel that was built to double up as a nuclear shelter for up to 20,000 people. Blast doors at the entrance weigh 350 tons...but take 24 hours to close.

Household Goods in 1987

The shelves, fridges and freezers are piled high with convenience foods. What did we do with all that extra time we'd saved? First, dig out the indigestion tablets. Then tackle a spot of DIY and finally move house, it seems!

Squash racket
The classic eighties sport. Prince Philip played squash to relax while Queen Elizabeth II was in labour with Prince Charles.

Muesli

Spaghetti

Jam doughnuts

Swiss roll

Beefburgers

Mince

Garlic sausage

Frozen prawns

Brie

Red Leicester
Originally called Leicestershire Cheese, the cheese was renamed Red Leicester after World War II to differentiate it from 'White Leicester' made during rationing when the use of colouring agents was banned.

Conifer

Frozen curry and rice

Fish and chips
Synonymous with British cuisine and described by Winston Churchill as 'the good companions', fish and chips were exempt from rationing during World War II, as the government feared any limitations would damage the morale of the nation.

VHS recorder

Ready mixed filler

Home telephone
The popularity of mobile phones has led to a decrease of landlines. Only 73% of British households had a landline used to make calls in 2020.

Fabric conditioner

Estate agent fees

Indigestion tablets

Books of the Decade

By our forties, most of us have decided what we like to read. But occasionally a book can break the spell, revealing the delights of other genres. Did any of these newly published books do that for you?

1988	Satanic Verses by Salman Rushdie
1988	The Alchemist by Paulo Coelho
1988	Oscar and Lucinda by Peter Carey
1988	The Swimming-Pool Library by Alan Hollinghurst
1989	A Prayer for Owen Meany by John Irving
1989	The Remains of the Day by Kazuo Ishiguro
1989	London Fields by Martin Amis
1990	Possession by AS Byatt
1990	The Buddha of Suburbia by Hanif Kureishi
1991	Regeneration by Pat Barker
1991	**American Psycho by Bret Easton Ellis** **Ellis received death threats on account of the violent and misogynistic content. He had to indemnify his publisher from being sued by his family if he were murdered.**
1992	The Secret History by Donna Tartt
1992	All the Pretty Horses by Cormac McCarthy
1992	The English Patient by Michael Ondaatje
1993	The Shipping News by E Annie Proulx
1993	Birdsong by Sebastian Faulks
1993	Paddy Clarke Ha Ha Ha by Roddy Doyle
1994	A Suitable Boy by Vikram Seth
1994	Snow Falling on Cedars by David Guterson
1995	A Fine Balance by Rohinton Mistry
1996	Infinite Jest by David Foster Wallace
1996	**A Game of Thrones by George RR Martin** **The idea for the story came to Martin as a child through his pet turtles. They lived in a toy castle, and he pretended they were kings, lords and knights.**
1996	**Bridget Jones's Diary by Helen Fielding** **This novel began life as a column in The Independent.**
1997	Harry Potter And The Philosopher's Stone by J K Rowling
1997	American Pastoral by Philip Roth

US Vice Presidents in Your Lifetime

The linchpin of a successful presidency, a springboard to become POTUS, or both? Here are the men – and the woman – who have shadowed the most powerful person in the world in your lifetime. (President in brackets.)

1945-49	*Nobody*: after Franklin D Roosevelt died, his VP Harry S Truman was sworn in and served without a number two.
1949-53	**Alben W Barkley** (Harry S Truman) Barkley died of a heart attack during a convention speech three years after the end of his term.
1953-61	Richard Nixon (Dwight Eisenhower)
1961-63	Lyndon B Johnson (John F Kennedy)
1965-69	**Hubert Humphrey** (Lyndon Johnson) Christmas 1977: with just weeks to live, the former VP made goodbye calls. One was to Richard Nixon, the man who had beaten Humphrey to become president in 1968. Sensing Nixon's unhappiness at his status as Washington outcast, Humphrey invited him to take a place of honour at the funeral he knew was fast approaching.
1969-73	**Spiro Agnew (right)**
1973-74	Gerald Ford
1974-77	Nelson Rockefeller
1977-81	Walter Mondale
1981-89	**George HW Bush** He is only the second vice president to win the presidency while holding the office of vice president.
1989-93	**Dan Quayle** You say potato, Quayle said potatoe: he famously told a student to add an 'e' during a 1992 school visit.
1993-2001	**Al Gore** Gore won the Nobel Peace Prize in 2007. Two others have won: Teddy Roosevelt (1906) and Charles Dawes (1925).
2001-09	Dick Cheney
2009-17	Joe Biden
2017-20	**Mike Pence** In the 90s, Pence worked as a conservative talk show host.
2020-	Kamala Harris

Spiro Agnew resigned in 1973, the second VP to quit in America's history (the first was John Calhoun in 1932). He stepped down after being charged with tax evasion and taking bribes. He covered his legal debts with a loan from friend Frank Sinatra. In 1983, Agnew was compelled to repay $268,000: the money he had taken in bribes, plus interest.

Stamps in the Seventies

By the seventies, any hobbyist intent on keeping a complete ongoing collection needed deep pockets (or a rich uncle). New stamps were churned out several times a year and the subjects became ever more esoteric: not just flowers and trees but racket sports, or paintings of horse races. Was your album gathering dust by then?

1970	Commonwealth Games
1971	British rural architecture
1972	Polar explorers
1972	Village churches
1972	Royal Silver Wedding celebration
1973	Plant a Tree Year
1973	County Cricket
1973	**400th anniversary of the birth of Inigo Jones** Not a household name by today's standards, Jones was an early and influential architect. He designed Covent Garden Square and parts of St Paul's Cathedral.
1973	Royal Wedding (Princess Anne and Mark Phillips)
1973	Britain's entry into the EC
1974	Medieval Warriors
1975	Sailing
1975	100 years since the birth of Jane Austen
1976	100 years of the telephone
1976	**British cultural traditions** The four chosen were a Morris dancer, a Scots piper, a Welsh harpist and an Archdruid.
1977	Racket sports
1977	Silver Jubilee
1977	Wildlife
1978	**Energy resources** In an era before renewable energy the choices made were oil, coal, natural gas and electricity.
1978	Horses
1979	Dogs
1979	Spring wild flowers
1979	Paintings of horse races
1979	150 years of the Metropolitan Police

More Things People Do Now...

... that nobody ever did when you were small – because they couldn't, wouldn't, or definitely shouldn't!

+ **Place a bet *during* a sporting event**
  This became popular in the 1990s; first on the phone, now online.

+ Turn on underfloor heating

+ **Buy soft toilet rolls**
  In 1942, a wonder was created in Walthamstow's St Andrews Road, one for which the bottoms of the world owe a huge debt: two-ply, soft toilet roll ('It's splinter-free'!). It was christened Andrex.

+ Talk to a smart speaker

+ Clean up dog poo (not doing it has been an offence since 1996)

+ Listen to a podcast

+ **Do a Sudoku puzzle**
  How many Japanese words do you know? Tsunami? Karaoke? Sake? In 2005, you likely added another: Sudoku (meaning 'single number'). The puzzle originated in the USA – but was popularised by Wayne Gould, a Hong Kong judge from New Zealand who found a translated version in a Tokyo bookshop.

+ **Cheat in a pub quiz**
  Which two capital cities mean the same in different languages? Who knows? Google knows, and a quick trip to the loo (phone in hand) is a modern phenomenon. (The answer is Sierra Leone's Freetown and Gabon's Libreville – but of course you knew that.)

+ Order something for same day delivery

+ Use chopsticks

+ Fly a drone

+ **Never watch live TV**
  Owning a TV but not watching any live programmes (just streamed content) might sound odd. But that is the reality for many – and around 1.5m have ditched the TV completely.

+ Eat in the street

+ Buy water

+ **Use SatNav**
  In the 1980s, Ronald Reagan permitted civilian use of satellites for navigation and opened up a world in which we never need to get lost again – unless we want to. Or the USA pulls the plug.

+ Argue for hours with strangers you'll never meet

A Lifetime of Progress

It's easy to lose sight of the breadth and pace of life-enhancing inventions made as you grew up – although some of these didn't stand the test of time! These are the biggies before you turned 50.

1969	Laser printer
1971	Email
1973	Mobile phone
1976	Apple Computer
1979	Barcodes
1979	Compact disc
1982	**Emoticons** The inventor of the smiley emoticon hands out 'Smiley' cookies every Sept 19th – the anniversary of its first use.
1983	Internet
1983	Microsoft Word
1984	LCD projector
1985	Atomic force microscope
1985	**Sinclair C5** Despite a body and a chassis designed by Lotus and assembled by Hoover, the ahead-of-its-time Sinclair C5 was plagued with problems including poor battery life, the inability to climb gentle hills and safety concerns.
1986	Mir Space Station
1988	**Internet virus** The first Internet worm was specifically designed to go after passwords. Its inventor was the son of the man who invented computer passwords.
1989	World Wide Web
1990	Hubble space telescope
1991	Websites
1995	**Mouse with scroll wheel** Mouse scroll wheels were developed primarily as a Zoom function for large Excel sheets but soon became used as a means of scrolling any kind of content.
1996	DVD player
1998	Google

The Biggest Hits When You Were 50

Fifty: an age when your musical taste is largely settled and modern music can lose its appeal...but how many do you know and how many do you like?

Never Ever ♪ All Saints
All Around the World ♪ Oasis
You Make Me Wanna ♪ Usher
Doctor Jones ♪ Aqua
My Heart Will Go On ♪ Celine Dion
My Heart Will Go On was written for James Cameron's movie Titanic. It went on to win Best Original Song at the following Academy Awards and sell around 18 million copies.

Brimful of Asha ♪ Cornershop
Frozen ♪ Madonna
It's Like That ♪ Run DMC vs Jason Nevins
Because We Want To ♪ Billie
Singer Billie Piper was only 15 when this song went straight to the top. She went on to swap music with time-travel when she became the on-screen companion Doctor Who, and to embark on a successful film and stage career.

Viva Forever ♪ Spice Girls
No Matter What ♪ Boyzone
No Matter What was originally written for the Andrew Lloyd Webber musical Whistle Down the Wind.

Millennium ♪ Robbie Williams
Believe ♪ Cher
Believe was the best-selling single of 1998. Unbelievable!

Gameshow Hosts of the Seventies and Eighties

What do points make? I've started so I'll finish. Shut that door! You can't beat a bit of Bully! The catchphrases echo down the ages from these much-loved TV favourites.

David Vine ⋈ (A Question of Sport)
Stuart Hall ⋈ (It's a Knockout)
Anneka Rice ⋈ (Treasure Hunt)
Kenneth Kendall ⋈ (Treasure Hunt)
Cilla Black ⋈ (Blind Date)
Born Priscilla White, the stage name of Cilla Black came about by mistake. Featured in the first issue of Mersey Beat newspaper, the journalist accidentally called her Cilla Black. Cilla liked the name and opted to keep it.

Barry Cryer ⋈ (Jokers Wild)
Nicholas Parsons ⋈ (Just a Minute, Sale of the Century)
Jim Bowen ⋈ (Bullseye)
After completing his national service in the bomb disposal unit, Jim Bowen worked as a teacher and was promoted to deputy head, but gave up teaching once he appeared on The Comedians alongside Mike Reid.

Mike Read ⋈ (Pop Quiz)
David Coleman ⋈ (A Question of Sport)
Prof. Heinz Wolff ⋈ (The Great Egg Race)
Bob Holness ⋈ (Blockbusters)
Magnus Magnusson ⋈ (Mastermind)
Angela Rippon ⋈ (Masterteam)
Noel Edmonds ⋈ (Telly Addicts)
Noel Edmonds has made headlines for plotting to buy the BBC, starting a pet counselling service, and driving a mannequin called Candice around in his black cab to dissuade the public from trying to flag him down.

Ted Rogers ⋈ (3-2-1)
Terry Wogan ⋈ (Blankety Blank)
Les Dawson ⋈ (Blankety Blank)
Larry Grayson ⋈ (The Generation Game)

Popular Food in the 1980s

Our last trolley dash takes us down the aisle at lunchtime, piled high with eat-on-the-go snacks and sandwiches. Stop on the way home for a deep pan pizza and a Diet Coke; end the day with a slice of Battenberg cake. Congratulations, you've just eaten the eighties!

Crunchy Nut Cornflakes
The cereal was invented in Manchester in 1980. Pity the poor Americans: it took 30 years for Crunchy Nut to cross the Atlantic.

Kellogg's Fruit and Fibre
Prepacked sandwiches
The prepacked sandwich was first sold by M&S in spring 1980. The range was small, conservative, made in-store and used whatever ingredients were plentiful (even if that was pilchards).

Viennetta
Trifle
In 1596, Thomas Dawson recorded the first recipe for trifle in his books, *The Good Huswifes Jewell*. It was essentially thick cream, rosewater, sugar and ginger. Jelly didn't appear until the 1700s.

Chicken Kiev
Vol au vent
Battenberg cake
Pizza
Pizza Hut claim to be the first company to sell food online – one of their signature pizzas via their Pizanet website, back in 1994.

Garlic bread
Kiwi
Sun-dried tomatoes
Potato waffles
Happy Meals
Diet Coke
Within two years of its unveiling in 1982, Diet Coke became the most popular diet soft drink in the world, and the third most popular soft drink overall behind Coca Cola and Pepsi.

Rowntree's Drifters
Hedgehog-flavoured crisps
Burton's fish 'n' chips
Chicken satay

Eighties Symbols of Success

In the flamboyant era of Dallas and Dynasty there were many ways to show that you, too, had really made it. Forty years on, it's fascinating to see how some of these throwbacks are outdated or available to nearly everyone, while others are still reserved for today's wealthy peacocks.

Car phone
Dishwasher
Children at private school
Waterbed
The modern-day waterbed was designed by a US student for his master's thesis project. Original fillings included corn syrup, and then jelly, before he settled on water. They were popular but problematic due to their weight and susceptibility to puncture, as Edward Scissorhands found out.

Second cars
Holidays abroad
Conservatory
Pony
Colour TV
Diamonds
Cordless phone
Birkin bag
A chance encounter between Hermès Executive Chairman Jean-Louis Dumas and Jane Birkin on a plane inspired the Birkin bag. The contents of Birkin's bag spilled out, and Dumas suggested she needed a bag with pockets, so Birkin sketched her idea on a sick bag.

Double glazing
Rolex watch
Leather Filofax
Mont Blanc pen
Newton's Cradle desk toy
Named after Isaac Newton and the cat's cradle, an early version was wooden, expensive and sold at Harrods. Chrome imitations followed. TV programme Myth Busters built a supersized cradle with concrete-filled chrome wrecking balls… it didn't work.

Stone cladding

The first UK car phone call was made in 1959 from outside the Lymm Hotel in Cheshire; human operators were used to connect calls until the 1980s. John Lennon wrote the lyrics for I'm Only Sleeping on the back of a car phone demand letter.

Cars of the 1980s

Many cars you might associate with the eighties were on the road long before then, from the Ford Granada and Escort to the Porsche 911. But this is the decade they arguably hit their stride alongside other automotive icons.

Toyota Corolla
Introduced in 1966, the Toyota Corolla became the best-selling car worldwide by 1974. The car was named after a ring of petals.

Volvo 240

BMW 3 Series

Volkswagen Golf
Sold as the Rabbit in the US and the Caribe in Mexico.

Volkswagen Passat

Vauxhall Astra

Triumph Acclaim

Porsche 911
Originally the Porsche 901 on its 1964 debut, the name was changed after Peugeot claimed they had exclusive rights to naming cars with three digits and a zero in the middle.

Jaguar XJS

Nissan Micra

Peugeot 205

Austin Maestro

Vauxhall Nova
The Vauxhall Nova inspired a series of comical bumper stickers, including 'You've been Novataken', and 'Vauxhall Casanova'. It was called the Corsa everywhere but Britain where it sounded too much like the word 'coarser'. It was renamed anyway in 1993.

Ford Sierra
Neil Kinnock had one of the first Sierras. He wrecked it in a crash.

Austin Montego

Volkswagen Polo

Austin Metro
Promoted with comical adverts, the car became one of the best-selling cars in UK history, and even Princess Diana owned one.

Ford Fiesta
The Fiesta is the UK's best-selling car of all time.

Vauxhall Cavalier

Eighties TV Gameshows

By the eighties, new formats aimed at youngsters - your youngsters? - were introduced. Some shows went digital or took to the skies; others kept it (very) simple, and a few remain family favourites to this day.

The Adventure Game

Treasure Hunt

Blind Date

The pilot episode of Blind Date was hosted by Duncan Norvelle, but he was quickly replaced by Cilla Black. Black presented the entire original run of the series for eighteen years, before unexpectedly announcing her departure on the show's first ever live episode.

Surprise Surprise

Countdown

Catchphrase

Blockbusters

Telly Addicts

3-2-1

The show's mascot and booby prize, Dusty Bin, cost around £10,000 to build. He was built by visual effects engineer Ian Rowley, who also operated Dusty Bin in the studio.

Blankety Blank

Bob's Full House

The instantly recognisable scoreboard was dubbed Mr Babbage by original host Bob Monkhouse. This was a nod to Charles Babbage, the inventor of the first programmable computer. In the reboot, Mr Babbage was replaced with a colour scoreboard, but the original board soon returned.

Bullseye

Cheggers Plays Pop

Family Fortunes

The Great Egg Race

Give Us a Clue

The Krypton Factor

Play Your Cards Right

The Price is Right

The Pyramid Game

Popular Girls' Names

Of the fifty names that made the Top 10 from 1900-74, only four have appeared since: Claire, Emma, Samantha and Sarah. (Oddly, names beginning with 'D' are now a rarity with no Top 10 entries in the last fifty years!)

Olivia

Along with other names ending in 'a', Olivia rose to popularity in the late nineties and has remained a favourite ever since. She's been number one or two from 2008 to the present day.

Ruby
Emily
Grace
Jessica
Chloe
Sophie
Lily
Amelia
Evie
Mia
Ella
Charlotte
Lucy
Megan
Ellie
Isabelle
Isabella
Hannah
Katie
Ava
Holly
Summer
Millie
Daisy
Phoebe

Rising and falling stars:

Emilia and Maryam: welcome to the Top 100!
Alicia, Abbie and Courtney: we're afraid your time is up.

Books of the Decade

Our final decade of books are the bookstore favourites from your fifties. How many did you read…and can you remember the plot, or the cover?

1998	The Poisonwood Bible by Barbara Kingsolver
1999	Disgrace by J M Coetzee
2000	White Teeth by Zadie Smith
2000	The Blind Assassin by Margaret Atwood
2001	Atonement by Ian McEwan
2001	The Corrections by Jonathan Franzen
2001	Austerlitz by W G Sebald
2001	**Life of Pi by Yann Martel**

Life of Pi by Yann Martel
When does inspiration turn into plagiarism? Martel was accused of the latter after similarities between his book and a work by Brazilian author Moacyr Scliar were highlighted, although Martel said he only read a review, and simply liked the idea enough to want to write his own version.

2002	Everything Is Illuminated by Jonathan Safran Foer
2002	**The Lovely Bones by Alice Sebold**

The Lovely Bones by Alice Sebold
At university, Sebold was beaten and sexually assaulted in a location where a girl had previously been murdered. Her experience and her subsequent reactions to it informed a novel called Monsters about the rape and murder of a teenager, later retitled as The Lovely Bones.

2003 **The Kite Runner by Khaled Hosseini**
Hosseini was inspired after watching TV news about the Taliban, who had banned the sport of kite flying.

2003	Vernon God Little by DBC Pierre
2003	Brick Lane by Monica Ali
2004	The Line of Beauty by Alan Hollinghurst
2004	Cloud Atlas by David Mitchell
2004	Small Island by Andrea Levy
2005	Never Let Me Go by Kazuo Ishiguro
2005	The Sea by John Banville
2005	No Country for Old Men by Cormac McCarthy
2007	The Ghost by Robert Harris

April 17 1970: Jim Lovell is brought aboard a helicopter, the last of the three astronauts from the Apollo 13 mission to be lifted from the floating Command Module.

Apollo Astronauts

Not all of those who have been to the moon are equally well known. Twelve landed; twelve remained in orbit. Gus Grissom, Ed White, and Roger B Chaffee died in training. BBC and ITV broadcast the Apollo 11 landing live, in the first all-night transmission. The landing was at 9.17pm, but Armstrong didn't take one monumental step until 3.56am.

Landed on the moon:

Alan Bean

Alan Shepard
Shepard was the oldest person to walk on the moon at the age of 47.

Buzz Aldrin
Charles Duke
David Scott
Edgar Mitchell
Eugene Cernan
Harrison Schmitt
James Irwin
John Young
Neil Armstrong
Pete Conrad

Remained in low orbit:

Al Worden

Bill Anders
Anders took the iconic Earthrise photo.

Dick Gordon
Frank Borman
Fred Haise
Jack Swigert
Jim Lovell
Ken Mattingly
Michael Collins

Ron Evans
Made the final spacewalk of the program to retrieve film cassettes.

Stuart Roosa
On the Apollo 14 mission he carried seeds from 5 species of trees.
They were planted across the US and are known as Moon Trees.

Tom Stafford

Popular Boys' Names

The most favoured names are now a curious blend of the evergreen (Thomas), the rediscovered (Harry), and those enjoying their first proper outing (Joshua).

Jack
This is Jack's last year on top. He was the nation's first choice from 1996 to 2008.

Oliver
Thomas
Harry
Joshua
Alfie
Charlie
Daniel
James
William
Samuel
George
Joseph
Lewis
Ethan
Mohammed
Dylan
Benjamin
Alexander
Jacob
Ryan
Liam
Jake
Max
Luke
Tyler
Callum

Rising and falling stars:
While names fell in and out of fashion in great numbers in the eighties and nineties, the pace has slowed. Only one new name: Blake. Out go Corey, Jay, Billy, Sean and Zak.

Things People Did When You Were Growing Up (Part 2)

Finally, here are more of the things we saw, we did and errands we ran as kids that nobody needs, wants, or even understands how to do in the modern age!

✦ Drink syrup of figs
✦ Preserve vegetables
✦ Save the silver chocolate papers from Roses
✦ **Eat offal**
Tripe was never on ration but long out of favour by the time the tripe dresser's fate was sealed in 1992, when BSE broke out.

✦ **Make a carbon copy**
Carbon paper was first patented by Ralph Wedgwood, son of Thomas Wedgwood, in 1806, for his Noctograph - designed to help blind people write without ink. The smell and texture are just a memory, but emails sent in 'cc' (carbon copy) might remind you!

✦ **Wash handkerchiefs**
You'd have to keep (and wash) a hanky for nine years to outweigh the CO_2 emissions of its tissue cousins.

✦ Use talcum powder
✦ Make a penfriend
✦ **Wire a plug**
Strip and route wires to the terminal; fit the right fuse. Not any more. In 1994, it became illegal to sell appliances without fitted plugs.

✦ Darn a hole in your sock
Refill your pen from an inkwell
Wind on your camera for another shot
See the bones in your foot at the shoe shop through a Pedoscope
Pluck a chicken
Smoke on a bus
'When will this fanaticism going to stop?' asked one MP in 1962, about a proposed ban on lower-deck smoking.

Scrape ice patterns off the inside of your bedroom window
Service your own car
Buy starch or blue bags for your washing
Play Spot the Ball
Spot the Ball was launched in 1973. More than 10 years passed without a jackpot winner as its popularity declined.

Printed in Great Britain
by Amazon

31895638R00061